FORGET NOT LOVE

ANDRE FROSSARD

Forget Not Love

The Passion of Maximilian Kolbe

Translated by
Cendrine Fontan

IGNATIUS PRESS SAN FRANCISCO

Originally published in French as
"N'oubliez pas l'amour"
La Passion de Maximilien Kolbe

Cover art by Christopher J. Pelicano
Cover by Riz Boncan Marsella

With ecclesiastical approval

ISBN 0-89870-275-5
Library of Congress catalogue number 89-81431
Printed in the United States of America

CONTENTS

To His Holiness, Pope John Paul II,
who, attentive to truth, to justice,
and to the voice of the people,
proclaimed the martyrdom of Maximilian Kolbe.

In September 1939, after the invasion of Poland by Hitler's armies, almost all the Franciscans of Niepokalanow had to leave their monastery. Before letting them leave for unknown destinations—for some exile, for others prison or death—Maximilian Kolbe said to them:

"Do not forget love."

I

The Mass in Red

Rome was beautiful, as always in autumn. The ruins looked like sponges soaked in sun, and the mild, motionless air allowed the pines to fulfill their decorative function in perfect immobility.

That morning, Father D. left the old Franciscan College very early to go to take the bus between the Pálatine Hill and the Tarpeian Rock. He had been invited to participate in the canonization Mass for Maximilian Kolbe at Saint Peter's. He prayed fervently that that morning his fellow countryman and brother Franciscan would be proclaimed a martyr by John Paul II, but he was not sure that his prayer would be answered; and while he waited for the bus, his gaze moving from the imperial hill to the rock of shattered ambitions, his hopes hesitated between joy and fear.

Father D. knew that right up to the last minute there had been difficulties posed by the experts. They cast no doubt on the sanctity of Maximilian Kolbe, whose heroism they had, moreover, acknowledged several years earlier. A man dedicated to the Gospel, imprisoned at Auschwitz, gives his life to save that of a fellow prisoner condemned to starve to death. Who could deny that he was worthy to be held up as an example and venerated in all the churches of the Christian world? But if the theologians definitely wanted Kolbe to be canonized, they intended that it be as a confessor, the ordinary category of saint, and not as a martyr. Consulting on this point, they had come to negative conclusions or at least dubious ones: although in August 1941 Kolbe had really performed an act of sublime charity in dying for another, he had not been interrogated specifically about the Faith by his executioners. That is the condition required in the traditional definition of martyrdom, and thus he could not be venerated as a martyr without a theological revolution.

Father D. wondered if John Paul II, even though his will carried the force of law in the matter, would feel bound by the opinion of the theologians or if he would pass over it to respond to universal expectation and his own desire.

It was Sunday, October 10, 1982. When Father D. arrived at Saint Peter's Square, two hundred thousand persons were already assembled; none of them knew any more than he did. The monsignori he encountered on the way raised their eyebrows in signs of ignorance. If there was no frustration in the expressions of these holy men, in whom the silences of the Vatican develop extraordinary faculties of perception, their downcast eyes showed something of the sadness of spaniels thrown off the scent. Confessor? Martyr? John Paul II, the genius of communication, had communicated nothing, and as he generally deliberated in his oratory, where God was his only confidant, his secrets were well kept.

The altar, banked in white and mauve flowers, had been set up in the usual place, at the top of the steps in front of the Basilica. Between the columns of the light golden façade a long banner was suspended from the balcony. At the bottom: the coat of arms of John Paul II, with the angled cross, its left branch protecting the tall initial of Mary. In the middle: a portrait of Maximilian Kolbe in the black robe of a conventual Franciscan, on a stormy blue background sprinkled with clouds that resembled white birds. Behind him was the glow of fire and in the distance there was a church framed by a rainbow. The upper corners were decorated with floral designs in white and red, which seemed to pose again the question: Confessor? Martyr?

No one knew anything, not the clever monsignori, not the dignified bishops, not the great crowd held in suspense within Bernini's marble pincers. It was only when Father D. entered the sacristy of Saint Peter's and saw red vestments for the celebration laid out on the table that he knew that Kolbe's sacrifice would be sanctified as it deserved. John Paul II, passing over contrary opinion, had proclaimed himself in favor of the verdict of martyrdom. Father D., after so much apprehension, could finally shed tears of gratitude.

In the square, the crowd found out only when they saw the Pope appear in red vestments, and after a moment of silence, there was a great murmur of popular ratification.

The ceremony was very beautiful and lasted from ten o'clock until noon.

After the entrance hymn, the three defenders of the cause, the Cardinal Prefect of the Congregation of Rites, the conciliar lawyer, and the Superior General of the Franciscans, approached Pope John Paul II to ask him, "in the name of the Church", to inscribe Maximilian Kolbe in the canon of saints.

The Pope did not reply right away. The people and the celebrants knelt to recite the Litany of the Saints; then, in the silence that followed, all rose to hear the Pope's reply:

"To the glory of the Most Blessed Trinity", he said, in a voice that seemed to stir the sea,

> for the exaltation of the Catholic Faith and the growth of Christian life, by the authority of Jesus Christ, the Apostles Peter and Paul, and by our own authority . . . after having reflected at length and listened to a number of our brothers in the episcopacy, we declare and decree that the Blessed Maximilian Kolbe is a saint; and that he shall be inscribed in the canon of saints and throughout the Church, piously honored among the martyrs.

The homily that followed began by recalling the Gospel: "There is no greater love than that a man gives his life for those he loves." John Paul II said that Kolbe had been granted the opportunity to carry out these words in an absolutely literal manner. It was impossible, he said, as if to justify his decision, not to hear the many voices of the people of God, impossible not to see that this death, freely accepted, rendered Maximilian Kolbe like unto Jesus Christ, model of all martyrs, who had given his life on the Cross for his brothers. It was impossible not to read in this sacrifice a powerful testimony of the Church in the modern world and, at the same time, a sign for our times.

And it is true that if theology can argue about martyrdom, love cannot.

During the Mass it was noticeable that John Paul II's thin face was marked by the suffering that time had not yet dispelled. The year before, only a few steps away, he had been shot by a hired assassin, and all the way to the hospital his white robe had concealed the blood gushing from his wounds. But after five hours of submersion under anesthesia, he had barely regained consciousness when he pardoned his assassin.

Thus, on that October Sunday, in that place where the

Church has always invited to pardon and called for mercy, one generous heart celebrated another. A convalescent of hatred gave to the world, as an example, a being of pure charity: the Martyr of Auschwitz, the saint of the abyss.

But who was Kolbe?

2

The Kolbes

He was born in the Polish village of Zdunska-Wola, January 8, 1894, according to our calendar. At that time Poland, divided between Prussia, Austria and Russia, found itself once more deprived of geographical bases and floating in the air in the form of a religious condensation in which, as today, faith and patriotism were one. It was one and the same thing to be a believer and to be Polish. The Catholic Church played at once the role of surety of Christian hopes and that of conservator of the national identity, at present without a country.

Baptized the same day, the newborn received the name Raymond, before being called Maximilian by his brother Franciscans, in history and in the catalogue of martyrs.

In the canonical process and according to the Procurator General (also called the Devil's Advocate, or according to that Roman courtesy that has taken as its unit of measure the radius of the dome of St. Peter's, the Illustrious Censor), his parents "shone as models of Christian life". From his pen, this is an extraordinary attestation, even if, as in this case, it is only a quote from the apostolic procurator at Warsaw charged with investigating the cause.

The Kolbes shone especially in their destitution, endured without bitterness and even with a certain gratitude for the uplifting effect that it had on their spiritual life. That was Maria Kolbe's point of view and, in consequence, her husband's. They did not even have a soft, caramel-colored suede family album to keep an engraved wedding invitation as a memento of their marriage. They had no such luxuries.

The father, Julius, a weaver, was tall, blond and good; that is about all we know of him. He spoke little, and, as he wrote even less, he has left nothing that would enable us to form a more precise idea of his personality. He was vowed to self-effacement, attracted for some time by Eastern spirituality; its techniques of personal abstraction appealed to him. He disappeared completely at the beginning of World War I; no one can say how. He may have been shot by the Germans or, as the Poles always have more opportunities than others to die, hanged by the Russians. The documents do not agree, but both hypotheses are plausible. A patriot, Julius Kolbe had long fought for a united Poland, which made him a target for the firing squads and the hangmen in all quarters of his divided country.

Maria, the mother of Maximilian—who was her second son—is better known to us. A photograph shows her at about age forty, dressed in black, with a flat-crowned black hat. The small chain closing her coat is the only ornament on her clothes. She is beautiful, with that beauty that comes, without fussing, from the interior unity of a being and that the features cannot belie. Her expression is pensive and kindly, and the infinitesimal trace of skepticism that we discern in it is certainly concerning only the photographer's camera at which she had been asked to look. The nose is straight and fine, and on the lips, highlighted only by their own shape, one senses rather than sees the appearance of a smile, like that of an angel in the night, passing at a distance, swinging a lantern. At that age Maria had already suffered much, and she would suffer more. But confronted with this face, in which the faith is clearly visible and which expresses so sweetly an almost infinite resistance to misfortune, one begins to feel that the martyrdom and the saintliness of the son had already begun in the mother.

As Maria was Polish, it is unnecessary to say that she was courageous. And as she managed simultaneously to fulfill the duties of a textile worker, a shopkeeper, a midwife, and the mother of a family, it is superfluous to add that she was lively and determined. She was essentially a religious person. As a child she prayed that God would let her die in time to avoid marriage, and she dreamed of entering a convent. But there were no Roman Catholic convents under the Russian occupation, no nuns, no monks. There were only husbands, and so she took Julius, who was gentle and whom she loved. They both willingly accepted poverty, but even so they had to avoid utter destitution—thus their rather complicated itinerary, following job offers and supplementary activities, until they came to the city of Pabianice, still in the Russian zone, the last stopping point in their family life.

Maria and Julius Kolbe had five sons. Two sons died in infancy. Books do not dwell on this sort of trial; all the same, it is one that lasts a lifetime. Maria wanted the other three to be perfect, and she raised them to this end, with a firm hand.

Francis, the eldest, was sent to school, costly as it was. Maximilian began by studying alone and later with the help of a priest. One day he requested a medicine by its Latin name. The pharmacist, astonished to find so much science in so small a volume, also took time to tutor Maximilian until he could be sent to school.

The Franciscans who passed through quietly, in search of vocations, noticed the two brothers, who seemed to be the most capable in their studies. They offered to take the brothers into their minor seminary at Lvov, in Austrian Poland, where Catholicism lived in a freer atmosphere than in the Russian zone. The offer was gratefully accepted, and the father took the two boys to the other side of the border, avoiding formalities, and put them on the first train for Lvov. He then returned home by the same route.

There remained the third son, Joseph, who at age twelve still needed his mother. But as he had already demonstrated an attraction to the religious life, his parents assumed that the Franciscans would later accept him as willingly as they had his brothers. On July 9, 1908, Julius and Maria Kolbe, anticipating themselves freed of the concern of settling their children, signed an agreement granting each other permission to enter the religious life. Such agreements are rare, but not as rare as one might think in countries where the Catholic Faith gains in intensity what it has lost in freedom of expression.

This agreement signed, Julius Kolbe crossed the border once more to go to the Franciscans in Cracow. After a year of effort, he realized that the conventual life was not for him, and he stayed on as a simple tertiary, that is, as a layman affiliated with the order.

In their turn, Maria and Joseph left Pabianice for the Benedictine convent in Lvov. There they were closer to the two older boys. Joseph went to boarding school, and then he too entered the Franciscan seminary. His mother became a Benedictine oblate and later took up residence in a Felician sisters' convent. She lived until 1946, and none of her children ever forgot what they owed her.

Little Joseph [later, Father Alphonse] was a discreet, faithful religious, of the kind who leaves only good memories when anyone remembers him.

Francis did not persevere. Leaving the monastery to fight in World War I, he did not return. World War II gave him a second opportunity to prove his love for Poland, once again overrun by enemies. He was arrested and imprisoned in a Nazi concentration camp, where he died.

The father, the two elder sons: the Kolbe family history was written on a war monument, with a line to the memory of two little children unable to survive poverty.

3

The Apparition

The witnesses seem to contradict each other regarding Maximilian's childhood. For some, among them his mother, he was a boisterous child, obstinate, independent—in a word, difficult. For others, he was a model little boy, the kind who is held up as an example in families.

But the disagreement is only apparent. The testimony differs according to whether it speaks of Maximilian before or after a certain event. With regard to this singular event, biographers usually dodge the issue, and the Devil's Advocate visibly tensed on his judge's bench.

This disturbing event, the sort for attracting the humble and setting the learned to flight, was a vision.

Such things do not get very good press. Religious writers themselves mention them only reluctantly, with infinite caution, when not preferring to pass over them in silence. Others devote themselves to giving natural explanations, with the support of Freud and neuropsychiatry. The most subtle speak of the momentary emergence of a sparkling, irrational element from the collective unconscious, like a piece of flotsam long held down by the soft vegetation on the sea floor, which reappears unexpectedly. The less gracious, who are also the least obscure, attribute visions and apparitions to hysteria, paranoia, simple hallucination, or obsessional neurosis, all the diagnoses putting the integrity of the subject in question.

But the great mystics are all distinguished by their stability and, quite often, by their practicality. It would be impossible to reply to malevolence more aptly than did Joan of Arc. If there was hysteria at her trial, it was on the side of the judges, preparing with meticulous pigheadedness a stake for innocence. After having recounted her marvelous story, Bernadette ended her life in a convent, hidden in those Christian thoughts born of silence and love inside their corolla of prayer. Teresa of Avila, who dialogued with Jesus Christ, still administered her monasteries with the good sense of a building superintendent. Ratisbonne, the unbeliever who saw the Virgin Mary one day in 1842 in a church in Rome, instantly learned about the Christian religion about which he had previously known almost nothing. He converted from Judaism to Catholicism, founded an order, and lived the rest of his life with no further revelations. Was he hallucinating? Teaching hallucinations do not exist. Kolbe was never in the least extravagant, unless it is an extravagance for a Christian to follow the Gospel. It was when he was thought to be dreaming that his reality, which encompassed the heavens and the earth, was more vast than ours.

Maximilian's mother, the only one in whom he confided, knew very well when her son had had the apparition. It was, she said, at about the time of his First Communion, which in Poland was made at about age nine. She told of the episode several months after Maximilian's death.

The boisterous, intractable child, to whom she had said one day wearily, "My child, what's to become of you?" had suddenly changed to the point of being unrecognizable. Meditative, solemn, he was often found kneeling at the family's little altar, dedicated to the Blessed Virgin, who reigns over all Polish homes. His temper had become milder, unless he had simply learned to control it. But he cried so much that his mother, at first filled with wonder at the metamorphosis, ended up by believing that he was ill. It was only through great insistence that she finally learned from the child what for so long she alone would know.

"Trembling with emotion", she said,

> and with tears in his eyes, he told me, "When you cried, 'What will become of you?' I prayed often to the Madonna to tell me what would I become. One day in church I begged her again, and she appeared to me, holding two crowns, the one white, the other red. The white meant that I would stay pure, the red that I would be a martyr. She asked me if I wanted them. I replied, 'Yes, I do want them.' Then the Madonna looked tenderly at me, and she disappeared."

During the canonical process, the Devil's Advocate, shriveled up by holy suspicion, spoke of the "presumed apparition" or the "supposed apparition". The Church looks at these mystical experiences with circumspection and takes her time believing in them. There were no witnesses to these extraordinary phenomena. The Devil's Advocate could only quote Kolbe, and as he did not dare summon the Virgin Mary to come to court, out of prudence and necessity he remained reserved.

However, if little Kolbe's vision is to be classified as an extraordinary event, the result is even more extraordinary. It will furnish us with the opportunity—and one hardly needs say how rare those opportunities are—to see how a promise made by God in the shadows of a church can be carried out in broad daylight by history, much later and as if by accident. These involuntary encounters between heaven's plan and man's freedom are a delight for a biographer.

For Kolbe would officially receive those two crowns, offered in a little Polish church, in the Mother Church of Christendom.

Kolbe's sublime end at the camp at Auschwitz soon attracted the attention of the Church, stirred by the veneration of the masses, and there was soon talk of making him a saint. This takes place in two stages—beatification, which permits limited veneration of the blessed, and the canonization itself, which extends veneration to the entire Church. These are two distinct steps, separated by an interval of some years, sometimes by centuries. Joan of Arc, beatified shortly after her death, was not canonized until 1925. It seems that in the meantime, among those who owed their homeland to her, no champion took up her cause.

Thus Kolbe, after the prescribed inquest about the heroism of his virtues, was beatified by Paul VI as a "confessor of the Faith" eleven years before John Paul II raised him to the ranks of the martyrs. There is no other example, in the canon of saints, of a change of category between the steps in a canonization. There are our two crowns. The proclamation of a confessor of the Faith is celebrated in white, that of a martyr, in red.

Little Maximilian's tears, as he told of his grace as one admits a fault, were the tears of a child forced to tell a secret who cannot control his emotion and who sees even as he speaks just how unbelievable his story is.

The mystical experience carries with it surprise, joy, and contradiction. The surprise is suddenly to have encountered a reality, unexpected but decisive, that is the ultimate reality, that before which all questions drop away because it is itself the reply, while the world is reduced to what it really is: an architecture of atoms built of snow, beautiful and clever but of a dubious reliability.

An authentic apparition is not a hallucination; it is not superimposed on the scenery; it is not a poster on a wall. It blows the wall away. Or rather, because there is nothing brutal or frightening about it, it opens the wall as one would part a light curtain. It imposes itself gently; it will be, forever, your only certitude, and all the rest, for you, will be an act of faith.

The joy that accompanies it is immense. Neither the body, nor the heart, nor the intelligence could contain it. It exceeds their limits to the point of abolishing them to the benefit of that faculty that churchmen called the soul in the days when they called holy things by proper names.

And it is here that the contradictions begin. The essentially undeserved joy is so great, so out of proportion with all hope, that the one it touches has the feeling that it does not belong to him. He will keep it a secret, not to hide it from others but because he feels that he does not have the right to do with it as he wishes. At the same time, since he cannot imagine that it is meant exclusively for his personal delight, he desires nothing so much as to share it, all the while knowing that it is incommunicable and sensing that no one will believe him. Thence the sort of hampered gait of the mystic, simple guardian of the gift he has received, who fears that he will be found unworthy of confidence placed in him and at the same time that he will betray beauty if he speaks—or charity if he does not speak. One foot in heaven, the other on earth, he will go on, all his life, limping to meet God without ever turning back, suffering because he cannot share it, convince others, or bring them along; restored to humility by his own impotence, had it not already been done by admiration or, even more likely, by gratitude.

The trouble with those who deal with apparitions from a learned position is that they have never had any. They are blind men denying colors. But those who have had the experience know the effects well, and they have often described them. First and foremost, it is a gentle revolution that reverses all the traits of the personality without changing its constitution. The violent become peaceful with the same force; the skeptical, enthusiastic, with the same critical sense, applied now to what they revered before; the proud will be humble, with that definitive humility that does not come from the sense of an all-powerful God but from the consciousness of his incredible generosity. Thus, after the episode on the road to Damascus, where he suddenly encountered the light of Christ, Paul of Tarsus changes direction like a source of energy changing its pole without altering its nature. With his usual taste for platitudes, the rationalist critic speaks of sunstroke; it is a rarity that sunstroke instructs you in a faith about which you know nothing, unless it disturbs your own; but the rationalist critic has his miracles, just as religion has its own. Thus, after Kolbe's apparition at age nine, his mother had the impression that he was completely different, and yet he was not. The forces of youth that he dissipated before in unruliness were suddenly united in prayer and charity.

Another effect of the mystical experience—I speak of true mystics and not of mystical counterfeiters who hold forth in various sects or hallucinators whose revelations teach them nothing—is the abolition of borders for the intelligence, which now roams, if I may say, without passport throughout the visible world and the immense invisible domain of the truths of faith, which is now tremendously concrete. All his life Kolbe would include the Christian mysteries not only in his concept of the world but also in his daily life and even in his administrative tasks. This astonished the religious around him including his own younger brother, appalled by his older brother's apparent carelessness in leaving to the Virgin Mary the responsibility of auditing his accounts. One cannot understand Kolbe if one disregards the vision that illumined his whole existence and made him one of those rare beings for whom everything is possible, especially the impossible, and whom nothing or no one can arrest, not even, as we will see later, those who imprisoned him.

4

Hesitation

There are three kinds of Franciscans: the Capuchins, who wear beards; the Friars Minor, who wear brown habits; and the Conventual Franciscans, who wear black. They are all sons of Saint Francis of Assisi, a filiation as difficult to honor as that of Shakespeare might be for men of letters. The little poor man of Assisi was a powerful genius. It is often said of him that he was the perfect image of Christ, a likeness accentuated by the stigmata placed on him at the end of his life like a divine signature. I see him rather as a little brother, in the biblical sense, a close relative of the holy family, somewhat whimsical, adventurous but faithful, dazzled by the older brother, and firmly resolved to prove that his gospel could be lived even in its seemingly unreasonable strictness. This son of the thirteenth-century merchant bourgeoisie, seized by grace, lived the parable of the lilies of the field, begging in his hometown, clothed in rags. He preached to the birds and to the fish; he sang of his sister Water, and his brother Wolf in his *Canticle of Nature,* which ought to have made him the patron of ecologists. It should be noted that the charming town of Assisi, which warms its picturesque remains in the sun of Umbria, having been ruined little by little by the competition between Flanders and Venice, has survived all these centuries thanks to revenues brought in by the reputation of the tramp who lived on its outskirts.

There is more than one common point between Francis of Assisi and Maximilian Kolbe. An initial miracle: from the crucifix in Assisi, Christ's enjoining Francis to build up his Church; for Kolbe, Mary's appearing to offer him the two crowns. They both had the same sense of the absolute, without compromise, reserve, or change of heart. It was rather disconcerting for those who saw it in practice. Francis and Maximilian had the same unbridled creative imagination. It was marvelously attractive to young people, and exceedingly disturbing for the sober souls one finds even among "the seraphic order" of Saint Francis. As we will see in the canonization process, these seraphs sometimes have a tendency to use their wings as armchairs. Francis and Maximilian had the same sense of poverty, seeing it as the most expeditious manner in which to expose oneself to the generosity of God. They shared the same chivalrous vision of man—a vision that we rediscover, intact and quite as misunderstood, in Pope John Paul II. Finally, they each challenged the world of their time, and this book is about that challenge.

At the Franciscan school at Lvov, Maximilian Kolbe was not simply a good pupil. To tell the truth, he excelled in everything, including good fellowship, but he was especially gifted in mathematics, physics, and science in general. He was a charming boy with a handsome face, always ready to help his little companions with the willingness of an obliging heart and the ease of one for whom difficulties pose no problems. He prayed much, almost always kneeling in the first pew, not to show off his piety but rather to keep from being distracted by the comings and goings in the chapel. He was cheerful and given to enthusiasm, but tears came easily to his eyes, especially when anyone mocked his German-sounding name as if to question that he was really Polish. His schoolmates marveled at his inventive mind. One of his drawings has been saved. It is a design for an interplanetary aircraft that was supposed to land on the moon or could be used to photograph the stars. It might have been flown, had the inventor had time to invent the fuel. Fifty years later several of his schoolmates were able to testify at the canonization process. Some had found him nice, and they had no more to say. Others still remembered the boy who wanted to know everything and who had followed his teachers down the halls of the school with his questions. They all remembered his extreme sensitivity, which led him to go through one of those crises of scruples that are a sort of spiritual nervous breakdown. He saw his imperfections as the terrible defects of one who should be excluded from eternal life. In those days one was cured of this malady by one's spiritual director. The treatment consisted of dissuading the victim from setting himself up as his own judge. Healed by what was essentially a cure by humility, he never again suffered this sort of ordeal. His customary elation returned, and with it the little personality trait that no one, neither his mates nor his teachers, would ever forget: his smile. It was a very sweet smile, like the first glow of dawn over a life dedicated to the light and so soon devoured by the night.

Maximilian's schoolmates thought him destined for a great scientific career. In spite of Maximilian's attachment to the Franciscan order, one of his teachers went so far as to deplore the thought that Maximilian's mathematical talents might one day be wasted counting the columns of a cloister.

But Maximilian wanted to be a soldier. When one has no homeland, the idea of dying for one's homeland becomes more vital than ever. And one has no homeland when one is a prisoner in one's own homeland under the domination of three foreign powers. Poland had nothing in common with her occupying neighbors except the religion she shared with Austria. And yet Polish Catholicism, which comes as much from Byzantium as from Rome, is very different from Austrian Catholicism, which is a left-over of the Holy Roman Empire. Poland is a country unlike any of her neighbors, even those with whom she shares origins and physical traits. Whereas the Russian is resigned, the Pole revolts, and the nationalism that makes the Prussian so disciplined makes the Pole so individualistic that he feels himself responsible for upholding, single handed if need be, the personality of his country when it is repudiated or oppressed. The Pole's history is composed of nostalgia and insurrections, as we see in the music of Chopin, when the gentle rain of sentimental, iridescent notes sometimes parts like a curtain to give passage to a hurricane of cavalry. No people has been so deeply Christianized. The waters of baptism flow through them like a river fertilizing the whole of their culture. Their Christianity was perceived and received like a title of nobility for all men. Thus, one sees how the chivalrous vision of humanity held by Pope John Paul II is so misunderstood by the Western middle classes, who long ago destroyed the genius of Christianity in favor of their Christianity without genius.

The whole Kolbe family was patriotic. How could Maximilian have been otherwise? His chessboard—he loved the game—was a battlefield. He launched military campaigns with his wooden pawns, or he erected defenses that would have rendered Lvov impenetrable had it not already been taken. The moaning of his dismembered country could not leave his young heart indifferent.

But the Devil's Advocate once again knit his brows. The Church has not placed patriotism on the list of virtues that engender sanctity. That is, in fact, what holds back the canonization of Father de Foucauld, in spite of the abundance of his spiritual harvest and the impressive number of souls who were inspired by him. Was he the saint of the desert whose conversion and spirituality we so admire, or in part, a supernumerary agent of French domination in Africa? Was he killed for his faith, and only for his faith? The Church puts mystics under observation and willingly sends the military to join them, be they heroes or not, in active service or reserves. The Devil's Advocate continued to wonder if the red crown, in what he imperturbably continued to call the "presumed apparition", was not in little Kolbe's eyes the replica of that "obsidian crown" that the Romans granted to defenders of the city.

Young Kolbe must have wondered also. To a sixteen-year-old, a military career seemed a more appropriate way of serving his country than taking a religious habit. His country was indistinguishable from his Faith. The problem was where to find an army that was not Russian, Austrian, or German, but rather Polish. But this sort of difficulty does not stop the young. He was so firmly convinced that his way did not lie through a monastery that he had succeeded in convincing his older brother, Francis, to renounce the idea also. In a way he became the first recruit in Maximilian's future army. Thus, when the good Franciscan Fathers suggested that Maximilian enter the novitiate to study for the priesthood, he asked for an interview with the Superior, for himself and for his brother, in order to refuse. It was on that same day that his mother came to the monastery to tell her sons that she was planning to live in a convent and her husband was joining the Franciscans. Kolbe recounted what followed much later in a letter to his mother, after his older brother had left the order:

> Before entering the novitiate, it was mostly me who didn't want to take the habit and who discouraged my brother ... then there occurred an unforgettable event: while we were waiting to be received by the Father Provincial to tell him that neither Francis nor I wanted to enter the order, I heard the bell ring to summon me to the parlor. It was you, Mama, whom Providence had sent to me in this critical moment. Nine years have passed, and I still think of it with fear and with gratitude to the Virgin Mary, instrument of Divine Mercy. What might have happened if, in such a moment, she had not stretched out her hand?

The audience took place. But instead of hearing his pupils refuse the habit, the Father Provincial heard them ask for it. I have already said that the older boy did not stay. But for Maximilian that timely bell that made him suddenly change direction sent him off with a running start. The rest of his life he was an arrow flying toward his target.

5

Two Letters

The good students were sent to Rome to pursue their studies. The celebrated Gregorian University taught them philosophy; the International Franciscan College made them theologians. In 1912 Maximilian, who continued to excel, was destined for the Gregorian University, but at first he refused to leave. He was eighteen years old, and he was afraid to go to Rome. He had been told that it was a city of perdition, populated by wives of Potiphar on the lookout to assail the little Josephs from the seminary. He wanted to keep his white crown. But since he had already made his temporary vows, obedience finally carried him along, and he accepted. He announced his departure to his mother in a letter written from Cracow. He had gone there to spend the two days of vacation accorded him by the good Fathers before the redoubtable expedition with his own father, whom he would never see again. He calls on his "very dear Mama" for help:

> I beg of you a special prayer, really the only one I need, because you will think of the rest, like the best of mothers. There are perils of all sorts out there. For example, I have

> heard that the women even tempt religious, and in spite of that I must go out and return from the university daily.
>
> One thing more, Mama; I want you to tell Beppino [his younger brother] that I ask him to think of me at Communion, with a prayer to Saint Anthony, no matter how brief. He wrote me that this saint has never refused him anything. He will listen to him now and protect me.

Maximilian's journey to Rome by train took two days and two nights. The young traveler admired the variety of landscapes revealed to him along the winding itinerary of his direct train. But he did not describe them in his letters to his mother. The outward world is necessarily beautiful and good, since, according to a beautiful line in one of his notebooks, "each thing is a small ray of divine perfection". But all these little rays together formed a sun that already dazzled his meditation and made his inner life grow. Nature is a mine of spiritual arguments, and at age eighteen he had already begun to exploit it.

Maximilian not only feared the Roman women but he also expected the worst on the part of the Roman men. Emancipated from the papal supervision since the proclamation of Italian unity, they were supposed to have sunk into an aggressive anticlericalism unknown in Poland. In reality, there is in Italy, as in all countries long dominated by the Church—however gentle that domination had been in the majority of cases—a long tradition of anticlericalism. One finds traces of it in the Italian cinema, which still blackens the caricatures of priests. But if that anticlericalism abused mockery, it did not use violence. After three or four weeks shuttling between the International, or "seraphic", College and the Gregorian University, Maximilian was reassured. He had not met any Messalinas or any priest eaters on the street corners.

> Very dear Mama!
>
> I only received your letter today. The mail is only given out here on Thursdays, our day off, and Sunday; however I had learned by chance that your letter had arrived on Monday.
>
> The situation is not as bad as I had feared. The Italians have better things to do than bother us. In any case, we usually go out in groups, and anyone planning to cause us trouble would do well to think twice.

He recounts to his mother the walk he had just taken with his mates, which led from church to church to the Coliseum. The ground there, he said, "is impregnated with the blood of martyrs, for which reason, in order to avoid profanation, one Pope ordered it covered with four and a half meters of soil". The path of today's martyr had for a moment skirted the enormous sinkhole of the cruel pagan games. As yet, no one suspected that they would be reborn in Europe, minus their talent and with the delirium of extermination.

In times past it was a convention among hagiographers that sanctity could be recognized from the cradle by the manner in which the infant virtuously refused the breast of its nurse, or accepted rattles only in the shape of halos. Since the progress of psychology and other inexact sciences, one would rather affirm the contrary. Sanctity comes with age, the combat, the laborious searching, and the agonized preference for perfection—that is, if it exists and if it is not just a form of pathological obsession that today we might rather tend to treat than to admire. One of the witnesses at the canonization proceedings, who moreover intended no harm to the cause, spoke of an "obsession". This expression was underscored with anxiety by the Devil's Advocate in his closing remarks. It bore on Kolbe's devotion to the Virgin Mary, but it might just as well describe his obstinacy about attaining the goal he had fixed for himself, which he summed up one day in his youth in this short phrase: "To be a saint, the greatest possible."

For Maximilian, to be a saint was the least one owed God in return for his graces, especially the grace of the priesthood. It is the recognition of a debt by a soul, conscious of its deficit, which, knowing that it can never discharge its obligation, carries out a sort of withdrawal from itself and makes a deposit to the account of divine charity. It is a fact that at the age of eighteen Kolbe was already no longer the owner of his own person.

Maximilian was "engaged" as much as one can be, and he organized himself with perfection in mind, with the meticulousness of a chief of staff organizing his forces. His notebooks consist of paragraphs from a veritable soldier's manual. The young man who wanted to be in the military would serve in the spiritual life. His first words in the notebooks are a call to prudence and humility, because he had the good taste to grant himself only limited confidence: "You do not have wings on your feet."

6

The Medal

At the Seraphic College, where Kolbe lived from 1912 to 1919, he left the same memory as at Lvov. He was remembered as a brilliant student whose grades continually threatened to break records. A tireless questioner, he pumped the wells of science dry. He was spontaneous, cheerful, though somewhat emotional and ready to weep when he thought he had deviated from the rule even slightly or when his confreres showed a lack of respect for it. This boy was already being observed with curiosity. He lacked the happy-go-lucky attitude of youth; on leaving class he went to chapel, and his walks led only to churches. One of his classmates, having heard it said that there was a saint at the college, recounted how he asked an Italian brother to point out the saint. Saints are not always visible to the naked eye, and the Italians, raised as they are in the canonization zone, are thought to excel in the appraisal of sanctity. Having seen Maximilian, he became quite attached to him. Sanctity is attractive at any age, and when it is young it is irresistible. Francis of Assisi was not much more than twenty when his former companions in revelry came, one by one, to follow his footsteps, on his new path, gathering *fioretti.* Bernard de Fontaine was twenty-two when he knocked at the door of Cîteaux with a squadron of young knights who had rallied to his spiritual genius. One can think that the testimony concerning young Kolbe, coming so long after his death, was colored, however perfect the good faith of the witnesses, by the terrible light of Auschwitz, which might have shone back from the hero to the child. I do not believe this to be the case. Moreover, we have testimony of the period, written, signed, and dated. In the college register on July 23, 1919, the rector noted soberly:

> Maximilian Kolbe, province of Galicia. Arrived October 29, 1912, ordained a priest April 28, 1918. Doctor of philosophy of the Gregorian University, doctor of theology of our college July 22, 1919. A young saint.

Filled with conviction to be shared, Maximilian was anxious to bring the whole world to Christ through the good offices of the Virgin Mary. His faith lived under the regime of a state of emergency. After the example of Saint Francis of Assisi's taking off to convert the sultan, one day he asked his superior's permission to go to convert the grand master of the Freemasons. The Masons were making a racket around the Vatican. They had unfurled fire-red banners depicting the dragon bringing down Saint Michael, as if to announce to the papacy, already stripped of its temporal power, the impending reversal of spiritual power. The era was one of womanizing and coarse jokes.

The superior, who was less impressionable than his pupil, knew how to persuade the latter that he needed to perfect his own dialectic equipment before challenging the "sultan". Maximilian acknowledged his wisdom, but he only postponed the project. The passion to convince others stayed with him his entire life. His religion seemed to him as beautiful as it was salutary, and in his eyes it was a sin against charity not to try to propagate it. He debated all the time and everywhere, in the street, on the train or bus, with the workers, with the hoodlums who blasphemed without knowing what they were saying, with the professor astounded to learn that this young greenhorn of a monk was a doctor of philosophy like himself, and, when he was ill, with the nurses and orderlies or the director of the hospital.

This zeal for converts would bring down on Maximilian's memory an accusation of anti-Semitism. This was based on a few sentences that proved nothing except that he would have liked to have seen the Jews at Mass, along with the Freemasons, the atheists, the Protestants, the agnostics, and the rest of the world. Before the Second World War, that is to say, before the great persecution (Holocaust), he certainly was indiscreet, but at that time it was not considered wrong to express publicly a desire for the conversion of Israel.

It was, in fact, commonplace to remind Christians that history, according to their Tradition, could end only in the winning over of the Jews to the Christian Faith. To speak thus today would be to pour acid on a people flayed alive. But one cannot judge Father Kolbe retroactively by the pieces of evidence furnished by the hateful, when he demonstrated so generously that this miserable sentiment had never inhabited the least atom of his being. The Jew was his neighbor, his brother, and he would have liked him to be even closer, that was all. Never, but never, was he lacking in charity. What is more, it has been established that during the war about fifteen hundred Jews found refuge in the community he had founded in Poland. Not all of them were saved, but neither was he.

From this most important part of Maximilian's life, from 1912 to 1919, we have few letters. Most of them were written to his mother at Lvov. She was, as it were, the family control tower, and from time to time he reported his position to her. Easter Sunday, 1914, regretting that he was not with her for the great feast, he tried to express a wish for her that would go beyond the traditional banalities. He could find only one: that she fulfill, in all things, the will of God, and he uses this curious expression: "God could not do better." Then he recounts, at some length, how he nearly lost a finger from his right hand as a result of an abscess. The treatment administered had not been effective, and, as the bone was infected, an operation proved necessary. It was then that the doctor, having learned that his patient had a little Lourdes water, the souvenir of a pilgrimage made by the rector, had the idea of using it. "And what happened? That next day, when the surgeon had planned to operate," Kolbe said, "I heard him say that it was no longer necessary—that I was completely cured." This unexpected cure interested Maximilian sufficiently for him to recount it, but what really astonished him was the grace, not the unusual phenomenon. For him, as for Leon Bloy, the miracle was "the return to the natural order".

During World War I, Maximilian's letters were rare, which is understandable given the difficulty of communication. He speaks much of religion and of the war only by allusion. But what could be safely mailed by a Pole, an Austrian subject, holding a Russian passport, writing from a country that had changed sides in 1915? He contented himself with wishing for peace, which compromised neither the sender nor the addressee. His superiors were perplexed; they sent him to San Marino until the war, or heaven, made the situation clearer, or until such time as he was granted a residence permit in due form, which he did not have and which was on the way. In this dearth of mail, where twenty months passed between the last two letters, there is however a triple mailing after the armistice in 1918. On November 26, 1918, he wrote to his mother; his older brother, Francis; and his younger brother, Joseph, all three in Cracow. To his mother he describes his ordination on April 28, 1918, at Sant' Andrea della Valle. This great Roman church has a most unusual façade; it is black surmounted on the left side by a beautiful white Bernini angel. There is, however, no angel on the right side; the sculptor was poorly paid and decided that he had done enough. Although Kolbe had been advised to make his letters as "light, light" as possible, he described the ceremony in detail so as to help his mother imagine that great day. At the end, having heard that Francis had not yet reentered the order, he asked him, or rather wondered aloud, what was the obstacle—the superiors, or his brother himself? That is the object of his second letter: "Write to me if you can (perhaps through Mama); let me know how you are, where you are living, what you are doing . . . and what your intentions are regarding the order." Maximilian asks Francis to recall how they entered the seminary together, how they passed their novitiate and were professed, and he hoped—in vain—that they would be together again, both in Franciscan habits, "to work for the greatest glory of God, for the salvation and the sanctification of our souls, and a great many others".

The older brother would not return. As for the younger, the recipient of that day's third letter, he was placidly following the path to the priesthood. Faithful and sensible, he would one day be somewhat disoriented by the religious activism of Maximilian, who saw the Virgin Mary everywhere—and consequently, saw difficulties nowhere. "Let us prepare", Kolbe wrote to his little brother, "to suffer and to work. We will rest after death."

Appended to the letter, which grew less and less "light", was a document that has become historic: the statutes for the first Kolbe foundation, the Knights of the Immaculata, created in 1917, before he was a priest. The project was stated on one page.

Objective: the conversion of sinners, that is to say, of the whole world [which of course included the "sultan"].
Conditions: consecrate oneself to the Virgin Mary and wear the Miraculous Medal.
Means: any, according to the circumstances of life and within the obligations of the Christian conscience. Of course, prayer to Mary, and the propagation of the Miraculous Medal.

This seems simple, and it is simple. And all the more effective; the members would one day be numbered in the hundreds of thousands. Maximilian hoped that, in the meantime, his younger brother might be able to translate into Polish the leaflet written in Latin and that he would distribute it in Poland. The little brother did nothing. He would always have much difficulty following his older brother, whom he did not understand.

I must speak of this Miraculous medal, which was the artillery of this Bonaparte of the spiritual conquest. It depicts the apparition of the Virgin Mary to Catherine Labouré, a young French nun, in the chapel of her convent in the Rue du Bac in Paris. I will quote her own description of the event from a book by Jean Guitton:[1]

> November 27, 1830, which happened to be the Saturday before the first Sunday of Advent, at five-thirty in the evening, after the point of meditation had been read, in the deep silence, it seemed to me that I heard a sound from the side of

[1] *Rue du Bac ou la superstition dépassée* (Paris: Editions SOS, 1973).

> the tribune [gallery], by the picture of Saint Joseph, like the rustle of a silk dress. Having looked to that side, I saw the Blessed Virgin at the level of the picture. She was standing, dressed all in white. Her silk dress was bright as the dawn, with straight sleeves and a high neckline. She wore a long white veil. Beneath her veil I could see that her hair was coiled around her head, held by a band of lace about three centimeters wide, without gathers, resting lightly on her hair. Her face was quite visible, her feet were resting on a sphere, that is half a sphere, at least I could see only half, and she held an orb that represented the world. . . .
>
> Her face was of such beauty that I cannot describe it. . . . And then suddenly I noticed the rings on her fingers, all set with gems, each one lovelier than the next. Some larger, some smaller, they all emitted rays. These rays fell from the gems, larger rays from the larger gems, smaller rays from the smaller gems, spreading out to fill space below so that I could no longer see her feet. . . . At this moment, as I gazed at her, she lowered her eyes to look at me. I heard a voice speaking these words: "This ball that you see represents the whole world, especially France . . . and each person in particular." . . .
>
> I cannot express what I felt and what I saw: the beauty and the brilliance, those beautiful rays. . . .
>
> A picture [frame] formed around the Blessed Virgin. At the top were these words: "O Mary, conceived without sin, pray for us who have recourse to thee", written in golden letters. Then I heard a voice saying: "Have a medal struck after this model; all who wear it around their necks will receive great graces. Graces will abound for those who wear it with confidence."

And sometimes for others, since Alphonse Ratisbonne was wearing a Miraculous medal when he was converted at Sant' Andrea delle Fratte. His bust now stands there parallel to that of Maximilian Kolbe, although he has not yet been canonized, for reasons we do not know.

The language of the mystic is not ours. In 1830, France had just treated herself to another revolution. The barricades had gone up; abstract ideas—Liberty, Equality, and Fraternity—were cried through the streets of Paris, which was left to the judgment of rifles; one king had fled in a carriage with his white flag and another had come hidden in the folds of the tricolor to surprise the republicans with a monarchy. At about this time a little peasant girl from Burgundy was leafing through the gleaming picture book on the walls of her convent. There was the unfailing talk of hallucination, as there would be about the apparition of Kolbe. But as I reread this text by Saint Catherine I can see only a great simplicity of heart, much conscience, and, before the ineffable, that touching application that makes a child wrinkle his brow and stick out the tip of his tongue as he tries to do his best on a particularly difficult drawing. The realm of the hallucination is not the mystical but the political, filled with wild discourses about a world that will never exist. Catherine did not hallucinate; Stalin did; he saw, just as clearly as I see you, slimy rats and lewd snakes right under his bed. And Hitler imagined—what am I saying—already fingered the fat Germany of his dreams, seated for a thousand years on the broken backbone of the inferior races.

Prayers and medals—such equipment may seem insignificant in a world long since at odds with heaven and a world that had not yet come out of the excesses of a great war that pure logic was incapable of explaining without the support of the irrational. Yes, what good were prayers and medals against the forces of materialism and those of the will to power, which, as soon as the peace was signed, would be back on duty? But Kolbe, intrepid in his faith, knew that spiritual weapons, which make so little noise, can be amazingly effective when he who proposes to use them also puts his own life on the line. And he had decided to do just that. In 1918, the day of his first Mass at Sant'Andrea delle Fratte, in the chapel where Ratisbonne's vision occurred, he arrived at the altar with eighty-three "intentions". Written out in a little notebook he had found in a drawer, they concerned his family, his fellow Franciscans and their order, the sick, the inevitable sultan, a Jewish woman, doubtless a secret convert, the Church, the world, his homeland. . . . And this, in Latin, which at once summed up his ethics and his actions, his existence and his thought: *"Pro amore, usque ad victimam"* (for love, to the sacrifice of my life).

Basically, that is the real definition of martyrdom.

7

La Casa Kolbe

At the foot of the Palatine Hill, history, who usually takes with her what she has made, forgot a few ruins. There, the crimson buildings of the "Casa Kolbe" face the wild grass of this scene of vanished glory. The former Seraphic College is constructed around a large space, which, unlike the recreation yards of our schools, with their chestnut trees planted in the tarmac, is a garden. There are paths, squares in the low hedges, and the palm trees waving their wild fronds over the rooftops. As we have just seen, it was here that Maximilian Kolbe lived from 1912 to 1919. However, it is no longer a college. The Franciscans now use it as their hostel, with a hall and a few rooms reserved for a museum.

On the second floor, Kolbe's room has been transformed into an oratory. In a corner, near a window, a glass-doored armoire contains a few souvenirs. The original statutes of the Marian "Militia" are framed, on a stand, like a menu at the door of a restaurant. The black robe of a Conventual Franciscan is suspended on a coat hanger. And there is a little reliquary.

It was in this room that Mary's "Militia" was founded in 1917. Kolbe explained how in a text published for the first time by Maria Winowska.[1] It was written at the request of a superior, and it is the only occasion when Maximilian wrote about himself. Usually he looked inward only to examine his conscience and never to contemplate the author considering his work.

> Much water has passed under the bridge. It has been almost eighteen years, so I have forgotten many of the details. But because Father Guardian has asked me to record the beginnings of the M.I., I am writing whatever I still can remember.
>
> I remember speaking with my confreres about the poor condition of our Order and its future. It was then this thought impressed my mind very strongly: Either put it on a better footing, or demolish it. I was feeling sorry for young men who came to us with the greatest intentions, but who soon lost the ideal of holiness they expected to find in the friary. But the thought of either bettering the Order or destroying it haunted me. How this was to be accomplished I had no idea. But allow me to continue.
>
> I remember when, as a boy I bought myself a figurine of the Immaculate for five kopecks. I always loved the Immaculate. Later on, in the Franciscan Minor Seminary in Lvov, where we heard Holy Mass in the choir, I prostrated myself on the floor before the altar, and promised that I would fight for her. How I would do this I did not know at the time, but I visualized fighting with material weapons.[2]
>
> Even though I had a strong inclination to pride, the Immaculata attracted me even more. In my cell, above the prie-Dieu, I always kept the picture of some saint to whom the Holy Virgin had appeared, and I invoked these saints often.

[1]Maria Winowska, *Le Fou de Notre Dame, Père Maximilien Kolbe, Cordelier* (Paris: La Bonne Presse, 1950), translated into English as *Our Lady's Fool* (Westminister, Md.: Newman Press, 1952).

[2]*The Kolbe Reader,* ed. Fr. Anselm W. Romb, O.F.M. Conv. (Libertyville, Il.: Franciscan Marytown Press, 1987), 147.

The Devil's Advocate is not always wrong. When he noted that patriotism and faith merged in Kolbe's devotion to the Virgin Mary, he was in the right. He was somewhat less correct when he saw traces of a military vocation in the idea of founding a "Militia", for Maximilian had renounced "material arms" when he took the Franciscan habit. In any case, if he was still dreaming of another uniform, his health would have made him unfit for such service.

> In the meantime, for the summer months and vacation, we moved from the Collegio to the "Vigna", a friary of our Order about a twenty or thirty minute walk from the Collegio. While there we played soccer for recreation.
>
> One day, while playing soccer I suddenly suffered a hemorrhage and felt blood come to my mouth. I stepped aside and lay down on the grass. My comrade, friar Jerome Biasi of happy memory, took care of me. I spat blood for quite a time. Then they took me to the doctor. I thought then that the end was near for me. The doctor advised me to take a carriage home and go to bed immediately.
>
> The prescribed medicine was very slow in stopping a recurring slight hemorrhage, which finally ceased. During this time the young and saintly cleric, friar Jerome Biasi, visited me often.
>
> After two weeks in bed, the doctor permitted me to return to the "Vigna", which I reached with some difficulty in the company of another cleric, friar Ossana. My confreres, upon seeing me, gave a very cheerful and noisy welcome. They brought me fresh figs, grapes, and bread. I ate heartily, and when the first hunger was satisfied, all my aches and pains seemed to vanish.
>
> It was then for the first time that I shared my intention of establishing an organization with my confrere, friar Jerome Biasi and with Father Joseph (or was it Peter) Pal, who was already ordained to the priesthood, but who was still my classmate in theology. However, I laid down the condition

that before we could act they were first to seek advice from their spiritual directors to make sure that this was God's will. . . .

So with the permission of Father Rector a first meeting or session was held on October 16, 1917, in which the first seven members took part. . . .

This was really the nucleus of the Militia Immaculatae (Knights of the Immaculate). This meeting was held privately under lock and key in one of the inside cells. The statue of the Immaculate, placed between two lighted candles presided. . . .

After that first meeting more than a year went by in which very little was done for the expansion of the M.I. In fact, some very serious opposition arose to the M.I. to such an extent that even members would not speak about the Knights among themselves. One of the members even tried to convince the rest that such a Militia was not needed. At that time also two of the members left our ranks to join the Immaculate: Fr. Anthony Glowinski and thirteen days later, friar Anthony Mansi. Both died of the flu which became rampant in those days.

My lung condition became worse again: I began spitting blood once more and had a very bad cough. I was suspended from studies. I used the time to rewrite the program for the Militia Immaculatae, which I presented to the Father General of the Order, the most Reverend Dominic Tavani, to obtain his blessing in writing. At the presentation, Father General remarked to me: "O that there were at least twelve of you!" He graciously wrote his blessing on April 4, 1919, and expressed his wish (I think it was at that time) that the Militia Immaculatae should be spread among our youth.

From that day more and more new members joined.

The real activity of the Militia Immaculatae in its first months of existence consisted—outside of private prayers—in the distribution of the medals of the Immaculate Conception, popularly called the Miraculous Medal. Here I must note that even Father General offered some money for the purchase of these medals.[3]

There were seven members: one of them soon ceased to believe, and several others no longer spoke of it, and yet this association, founded by an invalid—and at its halting beginning, weak itself—would soon prosper.

This text is, I repeat, the only one in which Maximilian speaks of himself, so all of it should be kept in mind. For example, his prudence sought the approval of authority before undertaking any enterprise. This conduct was doubtless dictated by a wariness of his self-confessed "strong inclination to pride", which he recognized as perhaps not just an aftereffect of his great crisis of scruples. And this strange joy that rose in him with the blood coming into his mouth and made him hope "that it was perhaps the end", as if to die at twenty-three in the middle of recreation was to be, in a way, chosen. Finally, he was certain that his companions, taken by illness, were in heaven, where they interceded for his work. For him there was no dividing line between heaven and earth. He went from one to the other without any difficulty, even more easily than he had once passed the frontier between Russian Poland and Austrian Poland.

In the glass case in the Casa Kolbe is a little silver filigree reliquary that contains all that remains on earth of Saint Maximilian's earthly body, lost in the ashes and smoke of Auschwitz. These are, to say the least, rather curious relics. The folder given out to visitors describes them as hair, but they are really hairs from his beard. In the 1930s, before leaving for Japan, Kolbe had grown a beard. This traditional attribute of the missionary was supposed to create a

[3] *The Kolbe Reader,* 149–51.

favorable impression on exotic listeners, on condition that the beard was sufficiently long to attest to the wearer's patient wisdom. Kolbe wore a long beard, with a few prematurely snowy strands. Back in Poland, he had it shaved off at the outbreak of the war. He was no longer on mission, and in wartime a beard on a young civilian always looks a little like a false beard. It was then that the barber at the monastery had the idea that today permits the faithful to venerate something of that vanished being; he kept the beard.

Thus, the intuition of a barber was far ahead of that of the theologians, who discussed Kolbe's merits and virtues through three volumes. Had he or had he not practiced faith, hope, and charity to the point of heroism? Could he, without error, be numbered among the blessed, and was he a saint? Forty-two years before it was agreed, the man with the razor, who kept the beard, had already decided.

8

A Sun

Every thought has its sun. For Kolbe, it was Mary. She illuminated his life, his heart, his intelligence, and even his death, as much as one can judge by the faint echoes that came from the starvation bunker: the words of canticles. This devotion was not exclusive, but it was permanent. Sometimes Maximilian's superiors found it dangerous to good theological order, close to obsession, illusory, marked by inconsistent sentimentality and frankly exaggerated. It worried even his younger brother, Joseph, who was astounded when Maximilian congratulated him on praying so well to the Virgin Mary when he had been kneeling before the Blessed Sacrament. All these grievances would be brought up by the Devil's Advocate, for the sake of form. He knew all too well that it is difficult to prevent saints from exaggerating, that is to say, from being exaggeratedly saintly. Saint Simon the Stylite, perched on his column and according to legend, nourished by a single cabbage leaf each week, exaggerated austerity. Saint Francis of Assisi exaggerated the parable when he explained to his companions that "perfect joy" would be, after a long voyage, to be welcomed nowhere and to spend the night in the snow and cold before a closed door. The saints bypass the limits all the more easily because they do not see them.

The number-one witness to this all-consuming devotion was a painted statue in the Franciscan chapel. Next to the small room with the relics is a large rectangular room whose windows open on the Palatine, which, from this perspective, resembles a wasteland, or rather a wave of terrain sweeping its imperial flotsam toward the sky and oblivion. At one end of the room to the right of the altar, beyond the rows of wooden pews, hangs a large painting depicting the revelation of the Sacred Heart to Saint Margaret Mary, in the rhetorical manner of the nineteenth century. Kolbe was often to be seen in front of this painting, but oftener still at the feet of a statue of Mary, which in those days stood on the altar. Dislodged by post-Vatican II changes, it stands today at a side altar. It is the Virgin of Lourdes, a statue which does not come under the heading of works of art but is part of the more touching category of objects of piety. The marble of works of art is heavy, smooth, and distant; the plaster of objects of devotion is light, humble, and appealing.

This Virgin with her blue veil wears her message to Bernadette Soubirous as a halo. If I may say so, she had a difficult time at the beginning when she appeared above a spring in the Pyrenees and proclaimed, "I am the Immaculate Conception." Religious authorities were reticent, civil authorities outright hostile. The prefect of police of the region spoke of hallucinations. The ladies of high society had great difficulty believing that anyone as prominent as the Virgin Mary could appear eighteen times in a row in the same dress. The psychiatrist consulted attributed Bernadette's vision to an effect of the light, which took the form of a blue statue, just as Ernest Renan, in that same positivist century, imputed the phenomenon of Pentecost to a draft. It goes without saying that Kolbe ignored these kinds of doubts or explanations. Mary, be it Mary at Lourdes, Mary on the Miraculous Medal, or most simply Mary in the Gospel, was for him, right to the end, a living person—and a mystery.

The heart of every Pole belongs to Mary. The Pole who stopped believing would soon stop being Polish. It is in his Faith that he finds his lost liberty. Moreover, it was at the citadel of Częstochowa that the seventeenth-century insurrection to liberate Poland began. It is as if the liberation of France in 1944 had begun at Lourdes. That is the sort of coincidence that reaffirms a belief over the centuries.

But Marian devotion is not the private privilege of the Poles. It is the touchstone and the measure of spiritual sensitivity for all Christians. The quality that the Christian soul finds irresistibly attractive in Mary is her humility within her incomparable grandeur. Mother of the Savior, she is without any doubt the greatest of created beings. It is she who opens the Gospel; she makes it possible by her acquiescence to the angel of the Annunciation. But after the shining crystaline canticle of the *Magnificat,* she is seen only in a sort of shadow or, as it were, backlit, a discreet presence who seems to recede into the distance, leaving the light scent of flowers on the pages of the Gospel. Christians do not venerate her as a mother goddess, as in pagan mythology. She is the worried Mother fleeing from the swords of Herod, her baby in her arms. She is the anguished Mother looking for her child for three days before finding him in the temple. She is the attentive, serene Mother at the wedding feast in Cana, who does not ask Jesus to perform a miracle but who obtains it by the subtle circumlocution of her banal observation: "They have no more wine." She is the Mother whose distress one can guess as she follows her Son, always at some distance, until that fatal Friday, when she cannot approach except to see him die. She stands at the foot of the Cross destroyed, before the stiffened body ripping itself from the nails, which have already pierced her heart.

A person, a mystery—such was Kolbe's "Immaculata". In Judeo-Christian history, Mary obviously had a unique destiny: virgin, she gave birth to the Messiah and, according to Catholic Tradition, she herself had been "conceived without sin", that is to say, exonerated from the stain of original sin that has soiled humanity since Adam and Eve. This is what Catholics call the "Immaculate Conception", which does not refer, as is often mistakenly believed, to the birth of Jesus, but to that of the Virgin Mary. It was thus that she introduced herself to Bernadette at Lourdes, by this mysterious appellation that theology has not even yet fully understood.

In one of his letters Maximilian wrote: "We know what 'mother' means. But we cannot grasp with our minds and our limited brains what 'Mother of God' means. Only God comprehends perfectly what the 'Immaculate' means.

"One can understand a little what 'immaculately conceived' means. But the 'Immaculate Conception' is full of consoling mysteries."[1]

Of course, to the modern mind, unaccustomed to the divine, this sort of photoelectric effect of mystery on the saint is very strange in the way that it absorbs the invisible and turns it into charity. It is that we barely grant God a

[1] *The Kolbe Reader,* p. 93.

semblance of probability. We would hardly dream of drawing our life from the mysteries of our Faith, which are no more than abandoned wells, overflowing in solitude. The mystery, this hard mystery of the Immaculate Conception, which easily sends sacred orators ricocheting into the ether of abstractions, was for Kolbe a formidable source of energy. It fortified him; it ordered his thought; it liberated him. And his view of the world was gently noble, the view of those whom nothing troubles, nothing frightens, who know where they have come from and where they are going. At Auschwitz, he lived only for her.

9

Four Pictures

Maximilian Kolbe had a changing face, or, rather, let us say that photographic plates did not always receive it in the same manner or with the same affability. I have before me four portraits that show us four faces where asceticism and sickness did not let youth last long.

In the first, Maximilian is twenty-four years old and a priest. Beneath the short, thick hair, the forehead is a wall enclosing armed thoughts, ennobled by an accolade of black eyebrows and shored up by the solid buttress of the nose. The cheeks are full, the jaw strong. The mouth, finely-drawn and youthful, looks not too severe to kiss a mother's cheek, something Maximilian's mother must not have often encouraged, but it is a mouth controlled by a tense expression and a terribly serious gaze. Behind the small eyeglasses, the eyes, brown or black, seem fixed, perhaps by the magnesium flash, and they look through the lens, through the camera, through the photographer himself at something unseen that demands an attention strengthened by discipline. This square face is one of resolution and character. One and indivisible, the soul is garrisoned there standing watch.

In the second photograph, taken a dozen years later, Maximilian's face has lengthened to a rectangle. The hair, cropped very short, is already gray and has receded to bare the forehead. Age has come before its time, and youth, having beaten a retreat, has sought refuge in the mouth, whose lips have kept their line. The head is slightly tilted toward the right shoulder, as was his habit. The eyes are turned toward the left, and one reads in them a general and encompassing benevolence; they are black coffee, but without any sugar. The gaze still penetrates the scene, seeking out the invisible. The peaceful physiognomy has a limpid serenity about it; it has never granted doubt or temptation a rendezvous.

The third picture is that of Kolbe at forty-two years of age. It is no longer of Maximilian. The forehead seems broadened by the effect of the sunken cheeks plunged in the copse of a full pepper-and-salt beard. The eyebrows are knit; the eyes follow an idea that has passed the horizon. The picture shows an old man, with a face gaunt from privation perhaps, from fever surely, consumed by the interior fire that his energy and his will never ceased to fuel. It is not surprising to find that such a person wrote one day in his notebook: "To be crucified for the love of the Crucified, that is the only happiness in this world."

The fourth and last picture is one of those identity photos where the lens did not spare the subject. Kolbe was forty-five. The disappearance of the beard had slightly rejuvenated the lower part of the face, and the mouth, so disposed to smile, shows here that seriousness suitable for administrative documents. The brow is wrinkled, and the deep furrows between his eyebrows indicate a high degree of concentration, or nearsightedness. The brilliant, dark gaze seems to pass over you and continues on its way behind you. In all the portraits, with only slight nuances, the eyes have the same intensity of expression; they blaze with zeal.

10

The Roaring Twenties

Kolbe left the college in Rome to pass from training to action immediately after the First World War. Europe was embarking on the Roaring Twenties, a sort of long period of relaxation that lasted from the bugle call of the armistice until the crisis of 1929, when the factories expired, their last gasps blowing the whistle on the recreation. Doubtless, the word that best describes this period is a word coined and used recently: *destabilization.* It was a time of political, social, spiritual, moral, aesthetic, and literary destabilization.

As soon as the war was over, the diplomats destabilized Europe. Noting the defeat of the Hohenzollerns, they proceeded to punish the Hapsburgs, reducing the dimensions of the house of Austria to those of a kiosk and the glorious double-headed eagle, its wings clipped and one head cut off, to the state of handicapped pedestrian. With this moderating element thus reduced to nullity, they mapped out a Czechoslovakia whose boundaries surrounded the most vulnerable elements of populations that were neither Czech nor Slovak but German and ripe for irredentism. They revived Poland by grafting on a piece of windpipe that crossed Prussia so that she could breathe the air of the Baltic. To give Poland new life was a pious deed, but the Polish corridor could only be for Germany a corridor of temptation.

Having completed their work of art, the diplomats proudly signed it. The setting was ready for the Second World War. However, amid a general unconsciousness and a lack of interest in lugubrious predictions, the Europeans strolled about through the ruins in a carefree mood, believing in a golden age and rapturously contemplating illusions, bathed in the glow of self-praise.

The society that emerged from the war was not the one that had entered it. Its morale had held up, but as soon as the armistice sounded, its morals, exhausted, granted themselves a holiday that became a leave of absence. One lived in a decorative universe of glass and metal that reflected the marked drop in the temperature of human relations. Perhaps it was to warm oneself that one danced the Charleston, that sort of gymnastic for skeletons shaken from strings. The syncopated music expressed so well the intermittency of wakefulness in the consciences of the populace. The muted trumpets sounded their pinched notes like ducks with their bills stuck in the mud.

This symptomatic dance performed in a state of bodily disjunction expressed in its own way the destabilization of the individual. Deprived of fixed points, the only way to avoid falling was by increasing speed—the first lesson of the bicycle. Mankind accelerated, and so did history.

The ordeal of 1914 had constrained the Church to leave her dogmatic fortress, from which, at the end of the last century, she had threatened to excommunicate all who spoke of getting out, calling them "modernists". During the war, the parish priest and the schoolteacher had found themselves side by side, half buried in the mud of the trenches. They had endured the same sufferings and spoken the same simple and curt language of survival. Survivors of the storm of hot lead that had beaten down on them for more than four years, they no longer regarded each other with the same insurmountable aversion as in times past. Clericalism and anticlericalism still had their activists, but anticlericalism had lost some of its virulence and clericalism some of its prejudice. The Church, having been compelled to compromise with the world, could not return to her citadel. But neither could she bring back to their senses those who meanwhile had discovered the dazzling fun-house of unconsciousness where good and evil had been abolished. The Church was not destabilized; she was put off center, pushed to the periphery of society, which explains the numerous exhortations she would later give to "go to the world". For centuries she had defined moral law, and those who had refused her that role had taken it on themselves, minus the divine references. Times had changed. The Church was sent into orbit outside the cities—and the minds. While the democratic governments strove to rear the Roaring Twenties like good fathers, the capital of moral energy amassed by Christianity in the course of its long history began to collapse. The West squandered its inheritance, falsified its values, and misappropriated its thinking in a sort of generalized relativism that crawled through doubt and ended up in skepticism. Poland herself was not spared. In the euphoria of the national resurrection, the spiritual tautness of the days of oppression suddenly gave way. The young people had not, of course, forgotten the Church, but they put off their thanksgiving.

It was at this time that Kolbe returned to his homeland.

II

False Start

In July 1917, a five-day journey brought Maximilian Kolbe back to a Poland liberated but bled dry. The country was minting lots of medals to celebrate her rebirth but even more money to fill her deficit. Four days of the journey were by Red Cross train. It was a good train; the passengers were fed and slept in beds. But it made lengthy stops everywhere, except at the borders, which it crossed without passport control. Reading Kolbe's letters to his younger brother gives the impression that he must not have spent much time at the window of his car. He does not say a word about the countryside or about his impressions when he debarked in the homeland he had left Austrian and returned to find Polish. All that interested him were the human beings and their eternal salvation, which meant that he lived in a perpetual state of emergency. Between Rome and Bologna, he undertook to convince a Jew, a draper, that the Messiah had come, that he was called Jesus Christ, that the Blessed Mary was a virgin, and that the hereafter exists. The rest of the catechism followed, augmented by the Miraculous Medal, which the beneficiary promised to wear. At Bologna, everyone got off. The Jew, who was traveling no further, went his way so well indoctrinated that he was already praying to Mary to convert him, if Kolbe's description is correct. Maximilian entrusted the draper to the Immaculata and thought that he would recommend him to the prayers of the Marian Militia. He got back on the train and encountered an infidel who openly denied the existence of hell before listeners dumbfounded by his temerity. For Kolbe, denying the existence of hell was denying the existence of the devil; denying the existence of the devil was denying the tempter in the Garden of Eden, original sin, the Old Testament, the redemption, and the Gospel: that was a lot.

So Kolbe took the floor, and "in the face of the evidence of reasoning", backed up discreetly "by a continuous invocation of the Virgin Mary", the impenitent publicly recognized the inanity of his argument. He returned to his compartment with the medal around his neck, like the Jew and like all who came within reach of the inexhaustible distributor.

At Cracow Kolbe was reunited with his mother, whom he had not seen for years. "You can imagine her joy", he wrote to his brother, "when I arrive unexpectedly at the convent of the Felician Sisters. She told me that she thought she was dreaming." She had raised her children with the severity of a woman who carries all the responsibilities of a poor family and the support of one of those devoted but ineffectual husbands who seem rather to serve as auxiliaries. But she loved her sons. And she admired Maximilian, who frightened her a little. When she learned of his death in 1944, she murmured: "I knew, I knew he would die a martyr's death." She had probably never stopped thinking of it.

Kolbe was kind and gentle, and he was mocked. He had a

superior intellect, and he was misunderstood. He was ill, and he was given two successive assignments that his state of health did not permit him to carry out. First, he was charged with the teaching of Church history in the seminary at Cracow where he had studied, but he was so short of breath that he coughed out his lectures. He preached, but he had no more voice than he had breath, and he did not have at his disposal the microphones that today fill the smallest public places with their crackling like stray crickets. The lack of compassion exhibited by his fellow religious is really quite astonishing. Here was a young man who, at the time, was given only a few months to live. He suffered from migraines and the fever of the malady that silently devoured him. His comrades called him "Brother Marmalade". It is hard to know whether they alluded to the sort of meticulous disorder of his room, which would have been harmless, or to his slow, soft gestures—gestures calculated to conserve his strength as he said Mass—which would have been mean. Or perhaps it was the sweetness of his Marian devotion, which, it is true, he was always ready to serve up, spread thickly. They joked about his disproportionate missionary ambitions and about his piety toward the Immaculata, which seemed to them improper and theologically ill founded. A dreamer, given to fantasy, a little simple—that is what they thought of this spiritual bomb whose fuse was already lit.

Most Christians had long since cut their religion in two. Down here is the earth, with its laws, customs, and conventions that form, along with a few Christian moral principles, greatly modified by indulgence, the basis of a reasonable conception of existence. Then up there is heaven, or what is cheerfully called "the beyond", to make clear that it is not down here and that, though one thinks of it and believes in it, it is the object of perpetual deferment. This separation of heaven and earth in which each exists in its own sphere and meets the other only on feast days is a very old metaphysical catastrophe. It has passed by many historians unperceived, and yet it helps us to understand why Christianity has never succeeded in being really Christian. Kolbe did not practice this kind of dichotomy. But the unitive vision of this man who prayed even as he argued could not but seem extravagant to those who did not experience the same attraction to the divine. The "pilgrims of the absolute" are as rare as Halley's Comet, and, when they traverse our atmosphere, those who watch them rarely have any idea of following them.

Maximilian could neither teach nor preach. That would be the only failure of his life. And this failure was due only to a switching error by his superiors. He made it his constant duty to obey them, the Devil's Advocate pointed out, particularly when he had succeeded in bringing them around to his point of view. Even so, those were not the only times when he obeyed. In a long letter to his younger brother, Kolbe sang obedience on a theme of angelic simplicity. The glory of God, he said, is the salvation of souls: no one desires this salvation more ardently than he does, and no one knows better how to assure it. Such is his will, to which we must conform, for our own good and for the good of all. How do we know this? Through his representatives on earth. Of course, "it sometimes happens that they are mistaken, but we are never mistaken in obeying them", because obedience gives us access to a superior wisdom that we would not know how to attain by our own powers. However, whether as an effect of Kolbe's force of persuasion or for some unknown reason, it is a fact that things had a tendency to turn to Kolbe's advantage.

Thus, freed from his courses and his homilies, Kolbe could

consecrate himself, with the approbation of his superiors and the bishop of the diocese, to his Marian mission and to the development of the Militia, which meant so much to him. And he succeeded. The mockers, doubtless tired, fell silent, and new memberships came from all over, from among his brothers in the order, from the university, from the towns, and from the countryside. Since not everyone had the same amount of time to devote, he established three degrees of engagement of progressive strictness. The first degree was for sympathizers; they prayed. Those in the second degree worked. Those in the third degree applied, or rather applied themselves, rigorously to the entirety of the statutes drawn up on that inspired day at the college in Rome. That is to say that one definitely took leave of oneself in the following act of consecration:

> O Immaculata, Queen of Heaven and earth, refuge of sinners and our most loving Mother, God has willed to entrust the entire order of mercy to you.
>
> I, N—, a repentant sinner, cast myself at your feet humbly imploring you to take me with all that I am and have wholly to yourself as your possession and property.
>
> Please make of me, of all my powers of soul and body, of my whole life, death, and eternity, whatever most pleases you. If it pleases you, use all that I am and have without reserve....
>
> Let me be a fit instrument in your immaculate and merciful hands for introducing and increasing your glory to the maximum in all the many strayed and indifferent souls and thus help extend as far as possible the blessed kingdom of the most Sacred Heart of Jesus. For wherever you enter you obtain the grace of conversion and growth in holiness, since it is through your hands that all graces come to us from the most Sacred Heart of Jesus.

The success of the Marian Militia is, of course, difficult to estimate. But the adherents were numerous enough from the beginning to ensure shortly thereafter a veritable triumph for the little newspapers that Kolbe published. He went straight ahead, paying no attention to criticism. However, his tuberculosis was progressing also, subjecting him to severe fever accompanied by hemorrhages. He never thought of complaining. None of Kolbe's letters reveal the slightest trace of bitterness, the least allusion to the injustice of the condition that enfeebled him when he needed all his forces to begin the execution of his immense projects. On the contrary, he accepted suffering as a supplementary grace and a means of action more powerful than all others. He did not seek it for itself—that would have been a pleasure—but to say the least, he submitted to it without complaint; he accepted it with gratitude. For he knew, with that active certainty of saints, that on this earth there is a secret cooperation between suffering and love. "When grace enflames our hearts, it calls forth a real thirst for suffering," he said, "for suffering without limits, for mockery, for humiliation, to be able to witness by our suffering to how much we love. For suffering alone teaches love."

Kolbe was a great mystic, and thus an incendiary who set fire to all wood, from the heavy crosses of sickness to the twigs of daily aggravations. And when stripped of everything at Auschwitz he had nothing else to burn, without hesitation he gave up what remained of his own body to the slow combustion of hunger and thirst.

12

Interlude

Maximilian Kolbe was sent to a hospital, and then to a sanitarium in Zakopane, a mountain resort where the population lived stretched out on verandas, like fragile plants in a conservatory. The journey, which seems not to have provided him with any opportunity for debate or use of his gift for apologetics, must have seemed monotonous. He had to content himself with shredding a handbill glued to the window of his car by missionaries from an American sect with the novel idea that they could woo the Poles by making slurs about the Pope. His first letter was to his mother: "Here I am, arrived at my destination. . . . And now, may God's will be accomplished, may the sickness remain, diminish, or disappear."

To his friend Father Pal, who lived in Rumania, Kolbe was a little more explicit: "Here I am in the mountains to recover my health. It is the same thing as in Rome, a pulmonary catarrh. I am supposed to walk only a little and slowly, to spend long hours stretched out in the fresh air, and to live as an exile, far from the monastery, for months." He worried about his companions in the Militia. He asked nothing more for himself than the words and music of the French song beginning *"J'irai la voir un jour"* (I'll see [my home] again some day). He reminded his correspondent of their mutual pact to pray each day at Mass to obtain "the grace of martyrdom". He made a date to meet him in heaven, after having expressed, however, his own fear of arriving there having let too many graces lie fallow. Such is the tone of all his letters; the philosophy is the simplest: "The best is what God wishes."

As Kolbe had only one lung left, and that one was not in very good condition, his Provincial had ordered him to ignore everything so as to think of only his health. He obeyed, but he did not have, how can one express it, the concept of systematic obedience, or else he had a different idea of health than did his superiors. In fact, when the religious at one of the sanatariums let him know that one of their patients was nearing his end, he forgot that he should "walk only a little and slowly". Day or night, he ran through the snow and against the wind, dripping wet, his hands like ice, to arrive in time, bringing the last sacraments to the dying. "Health", for him, was the good of others.

In these conditions, in this city on the edge of shadow, it was impossible for Kolbe to let many of the souls around him wander in the void of skepticism or be engulfed in the dead waters of despair. He was constantly on the alert, like a sort of paramedic amid these spiritual plagues. He carried with him not only his persuasive talents but also a smile that everyone found charming, and he went straight for the places where the peril seemed to him the greatest. He converted freethinkers and gained the interest of a Jew who asked to be baptized and received baptism from him without difficulty. He brought back to the Church, or very nearly, the director of a clinic who had long been away. He besieged the sanitarium of the university health service, peopled with young unbelievers, a breed rare in Poland, and ended up carrying them to the Church with him. He had posted a garrison of Miraculous Medals and reinforced his position with volleys from the Gospels. And he did all this without shirking his hours on the chaise longue, which he offered up in holy obedience.

Even though Maximilian did not take very good care of himself, his health improved somewhat. In the spring of 1921, the doctors advised him to spend the warm season in the country, and his superiors sent him to the monastery at Nieszawa. This time, the train that carried him was not as dreary a convoy as that to Zakopane, when only the meager handbill had been there to give him something to do. This train was a real horn of plenty, his car an enchanted carriage. He wrote to his friends in the Marian Militia in Cracow:

> On the way to Nieszawa I had occasion to speak with several different persons, a Jew (without side curls), a young Jewish girl (elegantly dressed), a Catholic from the Caucasus, and several others. I started the conversation on a religious theme, without much difficulty, and contented myself with intervening only when it was necessary to clarify some point. The Immaculata helped me to think clearly, and all went well.

When the train was approaching the station, Kolbe took the floor, summed up the conversation, and concluded with a brief exposition ranging from natural law and the choosing of Israel to Protestantism and Catholicism. He ended by saying that prayer is the best way of recognizing the truth. Everyone was pleased—the Jews to have been chosen, the Protestant not to have been reproved—and as they debarked, the Catholic from the Caucasus let Kolbe know how satisfied they all were. Such was his method, and such his idea of a pleasant trip.

At Nieszawa, for a start, Kolbe had to overcome a very great temptation. Very near the monastery there was a school where four hundred children lived in spiritual neglect. Holy obedience, of which he was reminded from time to time, forbade him to look after them. This was one of the sort of permanent duties that his superiors had forbidden him to accept as long as he was not cured. So he had to suffer the torment of Tantalus, like a sort of beneficent ogre passing each day by a reserve of unapproachable little Tom Thumbs. Was it perhaps to compensate for this disappointment that he besieged a Protestant pastor with deep, tricky questions about the Scriptures, in particular about the texts relating to the primacy of Peter, otherwise known as the Pope? Kolbe pressed the pastor so much that the man closed the front door on him, only to see him return by the service entrance. It seems that he had barely broken through the pastor's first line of defense when Kolbe learned, suddenly, of his own reported death! It is not known how the news of his death reached Rome, but it greatly dismayed Father Igundi, rector of the college. He was perhaps the first to guess what sort of duckling the old college had sheltered under its seraphic wings. Immediately, he had a Mass said for the repose of the deceased, and he wrote in his register: "June 14: Today a Requiem Mass was sung for the soul of Father Maximilian Raymond Kolbe, from the province of Poland, student of this college, who died of phthisis the ______. He was a little angel, a young saint, full of fervor and of zeal, one of the best students this college might ever have had."

In the blank space left for date of death to be filled in later, one can read, in slightly fresher ink, the exclamation that expressed the distress and the joy felt by the good rector: "False news! He is not dead!"

13

Blossoming

Not only was Kolbe not dead, but he was feeling better, thanks to the good air and to a collapsed lung that he never mentioned. He was putting the finishing touches on his plan for besieging the neighboring Protestant minister. He wrote to Rome to give news of himself. He also wrote to his younger brother, who had naïvely confessed that he felt himself very close to the priestly ideal when Maximilian spoke of it and very far when he read his letters. It must be said that these letters were not of the kind to flatter the illusions of a nice young monk. The further one goes into the infinite, the more of the path there is to travel. That is the first conclusion to which an aspiring saint must come if he is not to make the mistake of believing that he has arrived before even setting off.

On his birthday, Maximilian wrote to Joseph:

> Could you reach the spiritual heights of your patron, indeed, if God willed it, surpass them? For, in all things, progress is possible! And should I wish you the sufferings that were his? Without such fire, the soul does not catch flame; it does not shine; it sinks into the dullness of anonymity.

Maximilian's missives were like cold showers to Joseph, who replied to his older brother: "You have only to write to me and I find myself again at the bottom of the ladder."

One senses the disappointment of the child who was already out playing with his halo as if it were a hoop and who finds himself sent back to school. But he did not become discouraged. He was a fine boy. Perhaps he would even have become a saint if he had not been later outshone by the lightning of his phenomenal sibling.

A little before Christmas 1921, Kolbe, cured or not, received permission to return to Cracow. He went back to the Franciscan fold with a project that would arouse mixed interest within the order. He was no longer content with the door-to-door apostolate and the railway symposiums; he wanted to circulate a newspaper, as if to cast out a net. In the beginning it would not be a very big trawl; he would be casting over a rather modest range. In short, it was to be a small journal. The layout was already in his head. There would be a few pages; the paper would be the least expensive possible; the cost of composition would be minimal and the editorial costs nonexistent. It would bear a title so romantic that it would discourage publicity agents. *The Knight of the Immaculata* would, among other missions, fulfill the role of liaison officer between the various centers of the Marian Militia. The *Knight* would not tilt at politics. These lists were not for him. In this domain of the more or less philosophical, of incomplete reasoning, of lies, of general misunderstanding, in the worst of hypotheses and in the best he would tend to miss the ring—from an excess of detachment and generosity.

Rather than wade around in the swamp of current events, the *Knight* would bring its readers closer to the image of God—that image some carried within themselves without distinguishing it very clearly and others without even knowing it. For intellects clouded by the related strains of materialism and ideology, salvation could be found only in the Faith. The *Knight* would tell them so, in the language of chivalry, which is the language of prayer and honor. As for the editorial format, it would be devoid of useless complications. Kolbe's instructions to his contributors were short and clear. With his formidable candor, he told them: "Do not write anything that could not be signed by the Virgin Mary."

Kolbe was to encounter difficulties. In the religious milieu, the press was still considered an impure method of communication. It was one thing to write books, even though one was invited to engage in this dubious activity under the control of the hierarchy. But a newspaper, those words that rub off, those flyaway sheets, have wrapped up so much garbage that what they say has become synonymous with what they have contained; this vehicle of liberal thought and free speech, this almanac of the devil and breviary of futility—was it acceptable that an honest Franciscan squander his energy on pumping this sort of hot air? The old-timers pointed out that Saint Francis of Assisi had no newspaper. Kolbe must have thought to himself that Saint Francis had had no bicycle either. However, he certainly would not have rejected any means of making his evangelical music heard as far and wide as possible. Kolbe's superiors feared, above all, that the order would have to pay the debts that he would certainly incur. They warned him that they would not finance or cover the enterprise, but they would permit him to undertake it.

Kolbe went begging. He wrote twelve of the sixteen pages in the first issue. He printed five thousand copies and handed them out in the streets. The text sang of Mary and was more of an ex-voto than a metaphysical or moral publication. Not once during his life did Kolbe ask himself the question that haunts frustrated missionaries: "What language should one speak to make oneself heard by the man of today?" He did not suffer from these perplexities. He repeated what his heart said to him and other hearts heard and understood. The readers wrote in, sending donations that were immediately converted into subscriptions for the poor. The circulation increased, and the coffers emptied, just as the skeptics had predicted. Kolbe had only one kind of response to this sort of situation. After Mass, he stayed a long while, praying. Finally he raised his eyes, and there on the altar he saw a purse with a card pinned to it: "For my dear Mama, the Immaculata". It was the money to pay his bills, and the message was too clear for anyone to refuse him permission to take it for that purpose. I believe that it was after this episode that he made what he considered to be a very practical decision. He glued a picture of Blessed Joseph Cottolengo to the bottom of the old cardboard box he used as a cashbox, the condition being that Blessed Joseph show himself as little as possible. Cottolengo was the founder of a charity for the handicapped, and he had prohibited the use of a bank account. His refugees had had to live from day to day, and no one who worked with him was to concern himself with the morrow. This was the man to help Kolbe fill his cardboard box.

These methods, embellished by *fioretti,* only half pleased the Devil's Advocate. He deplored hearing the details of the wrapping described by the recipient of the gift. He would have liked Kolbe to be more discreet about his subsidies from the Virgin Mary, although he regretted that Kolbe had been too discreet about her apparitions to him. Also, the Devil's Advocate disliked Kolbe's way of managing his enterprise; it seemed utterly risky. The Devil's Advocate is demanding; that is his duty. He willingly admitted: "My responsibility is to purge the angels."

However, to watch him purging brings to mind the man who at Cana changed six enormous jars of water into wine after the wedding guests had already emptied the cellar. Would he be accused of a lack of temperance? Or the example he gave to his disciples of the lilies of the field that neither spin nor work: Would that be judged manifest imprudence? I cannot help but wonder if this austere tribunal that debates the cause of saints today would canonize Jesus Christ.

In spite of his new banker, who did what he could, Kolbe could not have continued for long to pay the printers. An American priest, charmed by Kolbe's ideas, which he found very good, made Kolbe out a check for one hundred dollars. This enabled him to buy an old hand-operated press from the Sisters of Mercy. It required several turns of the crank for each page, and the Sisters did not have the strength to operate it. The heavy mechanism exhausted even the most robust of the brothers assigned to turn it. Kolbe soon added a typesetting machine that simply appeared from an unknown source, appropriately enough on the Feast of the Immaculate Conception. Then there were his carboys of ink, his stock of paper, the comings and goings of copywriters and deliverymen, the postmen, the readers, and all of his books and manuals and paperwork—Kolbe was becoming cumbersome!

Kolbe was sent to Grodno, a corner of Poland where nature did not show her generosity, to a monastery on the verge of ruin. He set off without rancor, with two companions. One, a brother with a strong arm for the hand-operated press. Two days after his arrival, Maximilian wrote to his mother and told her how as he was trying to read his breviary by the light of the street lamp at the station, a Jew had offered him a candle. The Old Testament enlightening the New—the allegory awaiting the painter. The Jew was thanked, with the promise that he would not be forgotten at Mass.

As Maximilian's mother would worry about his health, he reassured her: the monastery at Grodno benefited from the good country air, his cell opened on the sunny side at noon, and the sun did shine sometimes. Kolbe would always take pains to convince those he loved that his lot could not be better, that he was fine where he was. Had he been sent to a glacier he would have extolled the charms of the igloo and the attraction of preaching to the ptarmigan. In one letter to his mother, Kolbe said: "Here, the people are good."

In any case, the depopulated monastery at Grodno furnished an ideal location for his press, his rolls of paper, himself, and his assistants. It remained only to be seen if *The Knight,* which had made its debut in the streets of Cracow, would enjoy "the good country air". You do not move a newspaper six hundred kilometers without losing some readers along the way.

But the result was the contrary: the circulation never stopped increasing. In four years it went from five thousand to sixty thousand. Later, when the Grodno monastery had become too small, it would be up to several hundred thousand copies, in addition to subsidiary publications. But this was achieved at the price of considerable privations. At the outset the little team had very little in the way of clothing or material goods. They still had to pay for their room and board at the monastery. Furthermore, Kolbe and his printers had to fulfill their tasks as good monks and take on their share of the ministry in the parish assigned to the Franciscans. It is hard to know how Kolbe's frail health withstood this schedule, and his letters do not tell us much.

To his brother, who before coming to join him was concerned about his health, Maximilian replied, in a third and final paragraph, that even if the fever often gave him a splitting headache, he did not have much time to be concerned with that sort of thing. What occupied him, day, night, with or without his head clear, was *The Knight,* now waging battle after battle. The machines, the typesetting equipment, the pounds and then tons of paper, the diesel generator that now lighted the monastery (to the glory of the Immaculata), the subscribers, those who paid and those who could not—it did not matter. Blessed Joseph Cottolengo was now submerged in sinking currency, as the Polish mark was being devalued as fast as it changed hands. And there were Maximilian's postulants, ever more numerous, knocking at his door to share what he alone could give them: nothing at all, and God.

This austerity, which worsened the privations imposed on all of Poland, brought the monks to the point of indigence, but it engendered neither bitterness nor melancholy. Men who have the audacity to set aside all social and material ambition and have enough divine practical sense to consider themselves with the required detachment can enter into a joyous variety of liberty unknown to those in the world. When the Trappist, no longer possessed of even himself, undernourished on boiled vegetables, passes us on his way from his work to the Divine Office, he lifts his hood to reveal a smile. And Kolbe did not have the somber disposition often attributed to those who contemplate the Infinite. He often regaled his companions with anecdotes brought from Warsaw, where the Poles consoled themselves with little stories of the disappointments in their history. In the evenings, when they had time and the weather was good, he would inventory the celestial vault for them. Or he would enchant them with some scientific tale from his own indefatigable imagination. For example, he would tell them that doubtless the universe had a memory, and that one day the growing precision of our instruments of investigation would permit us to leaf through it like a history book. We would then be able to see Christ just as he was on earth.

But it was not Maximilian's gift for science fiction that attracted the young; it was his faith, the limitless space in which his intelligence moved, the air that one breathes only in prayer, and the direct style of his apostolate. For he was not like these new theologians who periodically honor Christians with their doctrinal uncertainties. Religion is a response to the triple question of Gauguin's painting: "What are we? Where do we come from? Where are we going?" With the Church, Kolbe responded that we are God's children, that through sin we narrowly missed falling from his creative love, and that we will return to him through Christ and through Mary. The young priests in Cracow never missed a chance to mock their confrere, sometimes gently and other times not so gently. His personality seemed extravagantly naïve, his work insignificant, and his *Knight* too much of a Don Quixote to be considered in the great debates of the modern world, which revolved around the void like those powerful funnels in the sky we call "black holes". They were aimed at the intelligentsia, by definition inaccessible, closed as it was in the tower of its own refusals: the refusal to admire, to believe, to adore, sheltered from the tonsured behind the loopholes of suspicion. How could one touch intellects always ready to deny reason when it was too constraining and even, if need be, to deny themselves in order to escape from their own logic? While the young priests in Cracow thought about thought, Kolbe thought about the souls left by the ebb of Christianity in drought and neglect. He flung himself toward them as one throws oneself into the water to save another, without thinking of the attention one may draw.

It seems that Kolbe was better understood at Grodno than in Cracow. In any case, he was spared the mockery, and the superior was his ally for the rest of his life. Even so, some did not much appreciate his apostolic hurly-burly and wondered out loud if it was really advisable to harbor someone with tuberculosis. But Maximilian's illness endangered no one but himself. In 1926, a serious relapse worried everyone except him, and the Franciscan provincial sent him back to Zakopane. He went only out of pure obedience, and he said he was "ashamed to rest while others kept their noses to the grindstone". In his letters to his brother Joseph, whom the provincial had assigned to Grodno as his replacement—and who had been timid about accepting the job, wrongly feeling it to be beyond his competence—he speaks of his "militia" and his *Knight,* of an automatic folder, of type—and also of those priests who wanted to halt the development of the enterprise on the pretext of unprofitability. This provoked a sort of holy anger in Maximilian: How could anyone worry about profitability when the world was drowning? He spoke of his older brother, Francis, who had not been happy in the monastery and who felt no better outside; he hoped for a good confession from him, but it would not come. He talked of Saint Anthony of Padua, who sent zlotys to Blessed Joseph Cottolengo, of a thousand other things, but not of his own health except in the form of such brief notations as "the fever prevents me from writing to you at greater length" or "I've put on weight; my color is nice and rosy; only the fever persists." And: "The Immaculata can do as she wishes; myself, my health, my sickness are her property, entirely at her disposal." In forty to fifty letters, only a single observation about the weather: the sun in Zakopane was not to be noted for its exemplary assiduity, and the altitude permitted one a close-up look at the clouds.

After a year of treatment, five hours daily on the veranda, that is to say, exposure to the clouds, Maximilian was considered cured, and he returned to Grodno via Częstochowa.

The Devil's Advocate found nothing to exploit from this part of Kolbe's life; all the testimony was favorable, and the reports of the inquiry added little.

14

The Statuette

In spite of added work space that sometimes seemed jerry-built, Kolbe's team finally grew too cramped at Grodno. They needed to buy new premises, or better yet, a military camp in an area better suited to the distribution of a newspaper. However, this was beyond Blessed Joseph Cottolengo's means. The opportunity arose near Warsaw, at the edge of Count Lubecki's estate. In the work quoted in Chapter 7, Maria Winowska recounts the smooth dealing that led to the acquisition. Kolbe went to the place, with a statue of the Virgin Mary in his arms. Judging the place adequate, he installed the statue there, mentally inviting the Interested Party to take possession of it herself. Then he went to the count's steward, who set a price. The price was too high for the cardboard cashbox. Unfortunately, it was also too high for the order, which was not wealthy. The Provincial let Kolbe know. Since all things are God's will, Kolbe showed no sign of disappointment. He requested an appointment in the next few days with the count to let him know that he regretted not being able to close the deal that he had been negotiating with the steward.

Before showing his visitor out, Count Lubecki, moved by a fatal inspiration, asked the imprudent question:

"What should I do with the statue?"

"Leave her where she is", said Kolbe.

It was what, in bridge, is called a "squeeze", or in chess "checkmate", one of those situations one cannot get out of without losing the game. Indeed, the idea of expelling the Virgin Mary was intolerable to a Polish heart. But how could the count leave her in place, as Kolbe asked, without remembering each time he passed her that one day he had refused her residence. He would be condemning himself never to say another Hail Mary as long as he lived. Count Lubecki made a decision dictated by piety, reason, and generosity: he donated the land.

Henceforth the place bore the name Niepokalanow, the "City of Mary". There were only a few carrots growing there. They ate them as they put up a group of thin-walled huts ("permanent structures break the élan", said Kolbe). There was one for the machines and others for the editorial staff, the administration, the community, and the statue, who herself had purchased the land. The neighboring peasants volunteered to help the workers, whose courage and frugality astonished them. Inasmuch as their own limited means permitted, they improved the ordinary fare of the community, which was often reduced to bread and water.

We have no letter from Kolbe relating the beginnings of the City of Mary. He wrote only to postulants to give them a few suggestions about their clothing and directions to find the monastery. It was quite a way from the station, not far from the house where Chopin was born, and there was no bell tower to mark it. The most interesting letter is addressed to the Provincial at Lvov. In it, Kolbe explains the failure of two candidates, "the one with such beautiful handwriting" and "the one who knew how to embroider". These two fine boys had come to him desirous of leading a normal monastic life and not having understood that in the wooden barracks at Niepokalanow they would have to lead such a heroic though small existence. They were expected not only to live as good religious but also to conquer, for the Immaculata, "one soul after another, outpost after outpost, to bear her standard to the dailies, the periodicals, the press agencies, the radio stations, the institutions, the theaters, the cinemas, the parliaments, the senates, in a word, to all the earth. And to keep watch over that standard so that no hand might lower it." Then Kolbe realized what effect these proposals might have on the Provincial, who did not have "all the earth" under his jurisdiction. "Perhaps I exaggerate a little", he said. But he added immediately that it is necessary to exaggerate when one does not want to fall into mediocrity. One feels as if one is reading, a bit ahead of time, the famous slogan of the student uprising of 1968: "Be realistic; demand the impossible."

These barracks covered with tar paper on their wave of open space were a flotilla of Noah's arks launched in haste. Instead of endangered species, they sheltered the morals endangered by the triple deluge of ideology, racism, and totalitarianism. In place of doves, the team at Niepokalanow would soon release thousands upon thousands of paper birds over Poland—innumerable copies of Kolbe's periodicals, recovered and passed out again to others by the two hundred thousand subscribers to the Marian Militia in which no one had believed, even its founders, with the exception of Kolbe. The setup became more modern, the barracks grew longer, and the chapel was enlarged. In 1930, a hundred religious or candidates were leading the heroic although small existence of which Kolbe had spoken to his Provincial.

Some stood fast, others left, or rather fled, but on the eve of the Second World War they would number more than seven hundred. I do not know if the Abbey of Cluny in all its medieval splendor ever had so many monks. And all this had been undertaken without funds, without "market research" (yes, there is market research done today for everything, even religion), even without any preliminary donations.

A single capital outlay: faith. Kolbe did not ponder the world, nor did he go to the trouble of astonishing it with any doctrinal novelties wrapped in pompous discourses, which under pretext of going into depth send the reader to the depths. Anyway, he would have been hard pressed to do so. The witnesses at the canonization process recounted that he lacked eloquence and that he was easily disconcerted by an audience that did not know what to make of him or was interested in fine oratory that was not forthcoming. But when he had the chance to speak on the sole subject that interested him—on Mary and on that love which had chosen her well before she even existed to give birth to the Word of God—then his intrigued listeners underwent a strange influence. Little by little, they took less note of his words than of his face, which shone.

15

Journey

The City of Mary expanded daily, and Kolbe, who even equipped it with a radio station, dreamed of endowing it with an airfield. But he had not lost sight of the world where he should be raising the standards of the Faith. The Orient attracted him, like so many great religious minds who are fascinated by those lands and those peoples, unknown before they prove inscrutable and which seem to offer Christianity such a smooth, round, porcelain refusal. Or perhaps it was quite simply because he had met four Japanese students on a train and in exchange for the inevitable Miraculous Medals he offered them, they had given him four little elephant charms. The little elephants' vast ears seemed to him eager to hear Christ's message. In any case that occasioned a totally Kolbean conversation with the provincial:

"Do you speak Japanese?"

"No."

"Do you have the money?"

"No."

"How do you intend to do this?"

"I'll go to my usual patrons."

He meant, of course, besides the Immaculata, the saints who were close friends of the house and its funds, Blessed Joseph Cottolengo and Saint Thérèse of the Child Jesus.

When NASA's pyrotechnicists are aiming for the moon, they shoot in the opposite direction. Similarly, a Pole heading for Japan had to go west to go east, as he could not cross Russia. From January 1930 on, Kolbe journeyed a great deal, sending copious details of his travels to the community at Niepokalanow. "I chatter, I chatter", he said. But it was his way of making his presence felt among his own from time to time. At Warsaw he made the rounds of the consulates. Before the war in 1914 it had been possible to travel about in Europe, with the exception of Russia, with no more than your calling card. However, after the war, passports and visas were required everywhere, as if the countries realigned or invented by diplomacy wanted to be sure of their boundaries, and the others were anxious to show the solidity of theirs. Kolbe wrote that at the Italian consulate, his command of the language earned him an idyllic reception. The Czech consulate was brand new, like Czechoslovakia itself, and the visa could be bought at a counter as easily as a stamp. The French consulate, alas! was another matter. It was as sumptuous as it was badly maintained: the columns were marble, but the draperies were in tatters and the chandeliers dim, and the visa was the most expensive in Europe. The Austrian and German consulates charged practically nothing. Kolbe scribbled notes on trains and in stations, reproaching himself for what he called his prattling, which revealed a side of him not much seen before. He was a lively, lighthearted person, completely at ease with himself. At thirty-five he was still, in spite of hardship and humiliation—the word appears often in his letters—the child, delighted that at age ten he had been in the chapel and seen the apparition.

Kolbe tells how a Polish gentleman, who stood and bowed to him on the train to Cracow, immediately received a copy of *The Knight* and then sat down and read something else. Two students got on, and Kolbe did not delay in engaging them in a metaphysical debate. The gentleman listened attentively, but as soon as they began to say that some people did not seek the truth for fear of finding it and thus seeing their obligations, he took his suitcase and moved to another compartment.

After Cracow, where a Franciscan Father, moved to tears, had embraced Kolbe when learning that he proposed to publish *The Knight* in the Orient, Kolbe visited Vienna. There he was dazzled by the Divine Word Fathers' house. They had typesetting machines, offset machines, binding machines, washing machines, machines to knead bread, machines everywhere except in the Church. He remarked on all this splendid machinery as the train carried him to Rome, via Orvieto. He had a whole series of steps to take to obtain the necessary authorizations and blessings for his oriental mission. In the Roman offices of the Propagation of the Faith, fine young natives of India, China, and Japan informed him about their homelands. Forthwith they set to translating *The Knight* into Indian and Chinese, as Kolbe proposed to publish it on the way to Nagasaki. The bishop there was Japanese, and he would place fewer conditions on Kolbe's activities than would some Jesuit bishop along the way. When he checked the price of the trip, he found it too high. Hoping that he could do better in France, he went there. First stop Assisi, and from there, the home of Saint Francis, he wrote to one of the brothers at Fribourg. The postscript to this letter is startling, especially when one knows the end of the story: "Write me if you still persevere in your intention to dedicate yourself to the Immaculata, if you really wish to consecrate your life to her, to be consumed, and to show yourself disposed to shorten your own life *through starvation,* by exposing yourself, for her, to privation and the risk of an early death."

From there on, Kolbe's itinerary followed a logic not dictated by the advantages of short cuts. At Marseilles he adroitly negotiated his passage on the *Angers:* he would eat in third class and sleep in second. The date of the sailing was still some time off, so he went to Lourdes. He found the basilica graceful, but, built by human hands, it seemed to him less beautiful than the grotto "where prayer never ceases", and then in a grotto there is always something of Bethlehem. He had begun to let his beard grow to make a better impression in the Orient. At Lisieux, which was just next door for him, he visited les Buissonnets, Saint Thérèse's house. Among her personal possessions he noticed a chess set. He felt less guilty about liking the game now. From Lisieux he returned to Rome via Paris, Germany, Niepokalanow, and Vienna. At that time the direct line went that way. After having gotten the Chinese visas, celebrated Mass "in the church where the Virgin Mary appeared to Ratisbonne", and received one hundred dollars from the very Reverend Father General of the Franciscans, who regretted that he could not give him a million, he took off again for Marseilles. Finally, on March 6, 1930, he boarded the *Angers* with the four brother Franciscans who were to accompany him. He wrote to his mother to announce his departure. The charitable association that was putting him up in second class with a third-class ticket now opened the first-class music room to him so that he could say Mass. The class struggle was over; the ship was his.

At each port of call, Maximilian left post cards, like Tom Thumb leaving his pebbles.

To the Father Provincial: "Slight seasickness, but all is well. We eat four times a day."

And: "I have spoken of *The Knight* to the bishop of Port Said. He has asked me to stop here on my way back."

To his brother Joseph, the timid temporary at Niepokalanow: "The brothers [who were with him] write so much that I can refrain from going into detail."

To his mother: "Another thirty days of voyage. Pray for me."

To the community at Niepokalanow: "On the *Angers,* in the Red Sea, near Djibouti. Remember us at Mass."

To the Provincial: "The Bishop of Singapore has asked for twenty copies of *The Knight* in Chinese. I am writing to you from my cabin, on the China Sea. I will mail this card from Hong Kong: from there it will travel through Siberia. The Bishop of Saigon has nothing against our establishing a house in his diocese." And later: "Tomorrow, Hong Kong. There must be pirates there, as there are French soldiers traveling with us." A postscript: "We have left the torrid zone, and we are beginning to breathe more easily than in the tropics, where one can only drink and perspire." To Joseph: "We can distribute *The Knight* in Hong Kong, but we cannot print it." To the Provincial: "A Chinese benefactor has promised us a house." To the community at Niepokalanow: "Shanghai. The Chinese edition of *The Knight* is encountering some difficulties. All is ready; only the permission is lacking. This confirms the premonition I had at Niepokalanow, that is to say, that most of our problems will come from the European missionaries." To the Reverend Father General of the order: "Shanghai. It is as I thought; the difficulties related to the periodical are great, coming not from the pagans but from the European missionaries whose orders and congregations have divided China into territories where each of them has the exclusive authority.

For us, there is only Shensi remaining free, but it lacks any sort of rail or water transport."

Kolbe was studying the possibility of printing *The Knight* in Chinese in Japan and sending it to China. "But the Bishop of Shanghai would like us to open an office, and he asks that a priest remain there in residence." For the third and fourth times, Kolbe complained about these feudal missionaries fortified by their little walls of China. After having left two brothers in Shanghai, he reembarked with the two others for Japan.

16

Mary without Sin

At Nagasaki, the first thing Maximilian Kolbe saw was a statue of the Immaculate Conception in front of the cathedral. The native-born bishop had let it be understood that he would willingly welcome reinforcements to help him pasture his Christian sheep among the cherry blossoms. But he was away, and his vicar-general took a dim view of the newcomer. Franciscan journalists did not particularly interest him. However, when he learned that Kolbe had studied at the Seraphic College in Rome and that he had even taught philosophy, his attitude toward him changed completely. His Excellency was searching desperately for a professor to teach philosophy at the diocesan seminary and would be delighted to have found one. Kolbe was not as pleased, but if the Immaculata had arranged things thus, so be it. He immediately saw what he could get out of the situation. He would teach, and His Excellency would give him facilities he needed, a new Niepokalanow from which *The Knight* could be sent to China. And in fact the Bishop was so grateful that that is just what Kolbe obtained.

Even so, the beginning was harder here than in Poland

land. The run-down premises given to Kolbe and his two companions—others would come to join them—put up only a partial resistance to bad weather. They slept on the floor; the roof leaked; they ate on benches or crates. Kolbe's stomach rejected the food, as he said, "In the missionary's life, the difficulty is the food." While waiting to conquer the world, they were invaded by mosquitoes. "The only way to protect oneself at night is to hide under the covers, but then one dies of the heat." Later the poor Father became ill. In addition to his headaches and the habitual fever, he suffered from abscesses all over his body. He could barely walk, saying Mass on one foot supported by his brothers. One day he was picked up off the road, unconscious. In his letters we find not a line about these sufferings and troubles. He thought only about the tiny flock of Christians in Japan, fifty thousand in Nagasaki, less than one hundred thousand in all out of a population of eighty million. They lived with the memory of the thousands of martyrs crucified in their country during the seventeenth century. Kolbe's imagination took flight. He could see *The Knight* armed in Nagasaki, leap the sea, cross China, conquer India, debark in the Near East, speaking Arabic sometimes, Hebrew sometimes, to finally reach a million readers, friends, sympathizers, half the world's population.

In one month to the day after their arrival, the missionaries, who did not speak Japanese, brought out their first edition of the publication in the language of the people. Only one difference: the word *Immaculate* being untranslatable in Japanese, *The Knight of the Immaculata* became *The Knight of Mary without Sin.*

May 24, 1930, Kolbe sent this telegraphic exultation to the community at Niepokalanow: "Today we sent out *The Knight* to Japan. We have a press. Glory to the Immaculata."

Such was the magic power of this race of founders.

Throw them out into the desert with only the clothes on their backs, without a map, without compass, without tools, and you would see the sands move to build a cathedral around them.

They passed out thousands of Japanese copies of *The Knight* in the streets, respecting the local custom. Before handing the magazine to a passerby, his agreement was obtained by a ninety-degree bow.

The text had been written in Latin or Italian and translated by one of the Bishop's clerks, a Methodist of goodwill, whom Mary without Sin would finally win over completely to her cause. The rusty press gave the printers as many headaches as the one at Grodno, and it produced the same sort of articles as in Poland, with a minimum of transpositions (only as needed, as in the title). The formula was unchanged, the success identical. When one touches the deepest fibers of human nature, the vibration is the same everywhere.

The expressions of hostility and lack of understanding, which had grown fewer during the years at Grodno, resumed now with even greater intensity. Kolbe was reproached for the poor intellectual and literary quality of his publication. It was said that he set little store by Japanese culture. But he did not believe that culture went as far or penetrated as deeply into souls as did religion. He constantly took inspiration from the words of Christ: "Father, I thank you for having hidden these things from the wise and learned and revealing them to the humble and the little ones." Once more they denounced the "sentimentality" of his Marian devotion. He referred to the Virgin Mary as "little Mama". One of his former close companions jeered at this innocent habit in an article savagely entitled, "God the Father, Papa?

the Virgin Mary, Mama?" Kolbe suffered from this cruel lack of understanding.

At the canonization process, the Devil's Advocate added weight to the accusations of theological charges. The accused had spoken one day about the dogma of Mary as mediatrix, and it was not a dogma, at least not yet. He had written: "My life, at any moment, my death, where, when, and how, my eternity, all is yours, Immaculate Virgin; do with me whatever pleases you." He was outlining a Mariocentric program instead of a Christocentric one. At least it was not an egocentric program.

If Kolbe's way of expressing himself was sentimental, for one cannot imagine him keeping his love private, there was no sentimentality in his thinking, which was light-years ahead of that of his detractors. The dogma of the Immaculate Conception, which seems to imply a strange sort of anteriority to herself in the Virgin Mary, is rooted in the heart of the Blessed Trinity. It is a dazzling mystery that has a staggering effect on the intellect bold enough to fix its gaze upon it, and Kolbe was bold enough to do just that. It is a strong devotion, like Mary herself. The very young person who, when she visited her cousin Elizabeth, sang the *Magnificat* ("My soul magnifies the Lord, and my spirit rejoices in God my Savior. . . . He has regarded the humility of his handmaid; he has done great things in me") is evidently a power of the earth and the heavens. All who are devoted to her receive something of her light. When others look at such persons, they see only the statues before which they pray, and they judge them simple-minded.

For Kolbe, however, there was something more serious than these skirmishes. He was still lacking the rubber stamp that would validate an administrative detail for the Apostolic Nuncio. And there were the recriminations of the Canadian Franciscans, irritated by the new missionaries' trespassing on their territory. Kolbe's work was in danger; in high places there was discussion of ending his mission. He left, traveling back in the opposite direction, to defend his cause before the order's Provincial Chapter. This time, Siberia was willing to open the door to let him pass that way, and he arrived in Poland at the beginning of July 1930. At the Provincial Chapter, taking place in Lvov, there were only friends, but he still pleaded his case with unusual eloquence. He put forth that the Franciscans had had many martyrs in Japan and that it was important to continue their apostolate. The Christian community at Nagasaki was the largest in the country, and there they could count on the support of Bishop Hayasaka. *The Knight of Mary without Sin* had been sympathetically received, the circulation increased from one issue to the next, and they not only should continue publishing but also should found a Japanese Niepokalanow for the glory of the Immaculata and the conversion of the "pagans". Then he fell silent, and while his case was discussed before him, more or less kindly, he discreetly said Rosary after Rosary. His arguments carried the day (if not the Hail Marys). His mission was set on a firm footing, and he received the desired canonical blessings.

During this episode Kolbe wrote little. One telegram to his brother, Guardian at Niepokalanow, said "Japan is in danger—pray." To his mother he wrote that she should not expect to see him soon. A letter to his Provincial indicates in passing that the house he had asked permission to found virtually exists already. There is a piece of land, "with a vegetable garden already growing", that everyone has advised him not to acquire. But it is so undesirable that it is not very expensive. He has purchased it despite advice to the contrary. At the time of the bombing of Nagasaki in 1945, the shock waves, the flames, and the terror of the atomic bomb died out at the monastery doors, which opened to the orphans of the city.

With his reinforcements, Kolbe returned to Japan by the same route, across Siberia and Korea. They had brought provisions, and they made their own tea in the stations. Kolbe had left Niepokalanow at night, unexpectedly—the opportunity of a train, or the train of opportunity—and when he went to say good-bye to his brother, he found him asleep. He wrote to him from the first stop: "I did not want to wake you, I would have hated to do that, but I looked at you for a long while." He would never see him again. A short while after his return to Nagasaki, a telegram came like a rifle shot. "Joseph died in sanctity—all continues as before." Kolbe had left his brother in good health, and here they tell him, without any details, that he is no longer. The telegram did not tell him that Joseph had died in a few days of acute appendicitis, diagnosed too late. Paradoxically, the only trace of consideration found in the message is the "all continues", a strange condolence meant to reassure Kolbe about his work. Joseph, this gentle little brother who had been so hesitant to follow the formidable Maximilian and throw himself into the celestial abyss of his Marian cosmogony, had in his turn let himself be won over and swept away. He died in the middle of a novena to the Immaculate Conception. The news reached Kolbe the eve of this great feast. The bereavement carried that grace; he could say Mass for Joseph [Father Alphonse] in white vestments. "I received the telegram . . . ," he wrote to whoever sent it.

> However, after the first deep emotion, comfort slipped into my heart, for the telegram was sent during the vigil of the Immaculate Conception. . . . Perhaps the funeral took place on the feast day itself? So why grieve? It is evident that the Immaculata called him to be with her. . . . The telegram arrived here on the seventh, after Mass. The next day, December 8,

> the feast day, I celebrated Mass for Alphonse in white; I could not do otherwise.

His letter goes on at length, to the point that Kolbe has time to reproach himself twice for "blathering". It is the volubility that, after the first moment of numbness, follows a great shock. Hit headlong, Kolbe spun like a top, skimming over all the subjects of his usual preoccupations. He recalled that "holy poverty, the bottomless fund of Divine Providence", renders the Franciscan richer than the most powerful financiers. He asks, even so, for an account of things at Niepokalanow. And he rings the bell once more to sound the call to arms for the conquest of souls, before coming back to his brother. "I ardently hope to receive details. . . . But surely, they have been sent?" He wrote to his mother—only a week later, unless one letter was lost, which does not seem to be the case. "So it is. . . . The Immaculata has taken Alphonse to herself. . . . Glory to her for everything. I can imagine what his funeral must have been like, the very day of the Feast of the Immaculate Conception. I am still waiting for the details. I have received only the telegram."

In the correspondence that follows he speaks again of his trans-Siberian journey, mostly recollections of practical details. With the "Bolsheviks", you had to travel in groups of four, as the compartments in their trains were all for four. If you were only three, a fourth traveler might come in day or night and inconvenience the other three. If you were two or alone, it could be worse. During the trip to Poland, a young married couple had behaved, in front of him, in such a way that he had to go out into the corridor and stay there for the rest of the trip. When you were four you could close the door, pray, meditate, in short, for the eight days it took to cross the steppes, lead the life of a little religious community on wheels; it was ideal. He sent news to the Father Provincial in Lvov about the "pagans" (he meant the Japanese; the Bible would have said "Gentiles"). They had received his paper kindly, writing an article about it in one of their own, four pages of high praise in fine print. He had even received a letter on majestic letterhead from the "Buddhist fortress" on the island of Shikoku requesting a subscription to the paper.

The Japanese Protestant professor who had translated the issues of *The Knight of Mary without Sin* from Italian had translated himself into a Catholic. A doctor, professor at the University of Nagasaki, came to see Kolbe, "to have a conversation in German". The conversation turned to a catechism lesson; the doctor was pleased, as he had regretted for some time that he was so poorly informed about Catholicism. Two little "pagans", who had lent a hand at the press, later took instruction and asked to be baptized. Prayer alone, Kolbe said, sufficed.

And he spoke again of his brother Joseph: "He can now do more and better than when he was on earth to spread the devotion to the Immaculata." Glory to her. That is faith.

Kolbe was a mystic, and thus deeply sensitive, so he had some difficult times. In that tone of his, he takes up the lamentation of Saint Paul: "I do not do the good I desire, and I do the evil I detest". He did no evil, but in his view the good he did was not pure. He reproached himself bitterly for taking credit, through pride, for what might have been the work of the Immaculata. It must be explained that for a mystic pride begins when he loses a clear consciousness of his own nothingness, when he finds the canticle of Catherine of Siena interrupted in his soul. "You are wisdom; I am folly. You are beauty; I am only a sordid creature. You are life; I am death. You are who are; I am who am not." Just as we have seen that poverty "is the bottomless fund of Divine Providence", for the mystic, nothingness is a source of inexhaustible richness, the limitless kingdom of God's generosity where, for him as for Bernanos' country priest, all is grace. Pride is to forget this, be it only for a moment. But sometimes human weakness comes to the aid of humility. "How often", cried Kolbe in a letter to his Provincial, "has it seemed to me that I no longer had faith, hope, or even love! . . . So I feel only loathing for worries, difficulties, suffering, and I aspire to a lazy and idle tranquility", which, of course, he would never know.

Sometimes the clouds of depression darkened Kolbe's sky. He would weep when his intentions were misunderstood or when his work was endangered, as it had been at the order's last Provincial Chapter. The Devil's Advocate judged these tears incompatible with the radiant exercise of heroic virtue, having noted that Kolbe had often been seen "sad and anxious", especially when there was any question of ending his mission. "Thus, when his superiors did not share his views, the servant of God collapsed, proving a fragility in the practice of the virtues of strength and hope." Proof also that saints are men.

As a mystic Kolbe was also realistic and attentive to the details of everyday life. When priests and brothers were preparing to leave Poland to join him in Nagasaki, he sent them a little travel guide with suggestions for the trans-Siberian crossing. They should equip themselves with

> a large vacuum bottle for hot water, which could be obtained free in most of the stations, where there are small pipes with faucets marked kipiatok (in Cyrillic characters, of course); also, a small teapot; a package of tea to last nine days, opened, to avoid paying customs duties; sugar, cups, and spoons, so

> as to avoid the dining car where one has to pay handsomely to warm one's stomach.

In Manchuria, the conductor takes care of hot water: he is paid at the end of the line. In Japan, no more hot water; you have to get hot milk from young boys who call out *"giuniu"* (milk) on the platforms. On the boat crossing the Sea of Japan, one again finds water. "It is a good idea to take a ticket for the deck and sit on a bench there, for inside, in third class, the heat is unbearable." Bring along a blanket to sleep on—it obviates the costly rental of bedding—and a coat to cover up with at night "according to the custom of missionaries". On leaving Warsaw, change from religious habit to civilian clothes, and on the trans-Siberian leg, avoid being recognized, but

> before any official, state openly, "missionaries en route to Japan". In case of any difficulty, the password is "transit", which disarms customs agents, who then affix their stamps to the luggage, including any packages of priestly vestments and vessels. Nothing will then be opened during the trip across Soviet territory. However, since one has declared oneself a "missionary", one can without any problem, keep in a small unsealed suitcase, a cassock, a rosary, a crucifix, and a prayer book.

All of this was accompanied by maps and sketches of a station and a train compartment, showing how the seats lifted to reveal a luggage bin and the little metal piece that one should remove from the door at night to assure privacy. Kolbe pushed his minutiae to the point that he recommended that his brothers get up early in the morning, before the other passengers, in order to avoid having to wait outside the toilets. Mystics do have their feet on the ground.

It should be noted that, at this time, in 1930, Russia was not so secretive; the Iron Curtain had not yet come down on its endless frontier. One could enter and leave again without the risk of too many problems. It seems unlikely that today the word *transit* would have the same magical effect on customs agents or that it would suffice just to offer them your bag to stamp to convince them that they need not look inside.

At Nagasaki, the priests and brothers at the monastery press would soon number seventy-eight, and with a circulation of sixty-five thousand copies, the newspaper *Mary without Sin* would be the largest Catholic paper in a non-Catholic country. During this time, the brothers at Niepokalanow had constructed what they pompously called "skyscrapers". The most recent edifice was meant to shelter the enormous rotary press that one day would print one million copies of *The Knight* along with ten other publications. Priests and workers, other than the worker-priests, were all photographed in front of their industrial monster, oilcans in hand, like birds perched on an iron scaffolding. When these surprising pictures were published, they provoked a slight recurrence of the malaise felt in the order. Some of the members could not get used to modern techniques of communication, and they did not trust birds who preached. The content of *The Knight* was still the same: Marian meditations, news of the various Militia groups, columns that paid less attention to the news of the day than to the feasts of the liturgical calendar, expressions of gratitude to Mary, all fitted into a small illustrated tabloid. It spoke not of the earthly world but of the heavenly one, salvation, suffering, and hope, in short, of all the subjects that the press no longer treated, if it had ever treated them. This made *The Knight*'s conventionality quite original. Its growing audience came to it, in fact, not for what it hoped to hear of the surprising, the scandalous, or the sensational, but rather for the continual complicity with what forms the basis of human nature to which so little appeal is made: the need to believe, to love, and to hope.

From Japan, Kolbe continued to direct Niepokalanow. He wrote long letters to his brothers, talking about machines, land, or money, always reminding them of the fundamental principle of his financial system: "Whenever the Immaculata wants something, it is only logical that she will cover the cost of it." Or he would describe to them the benefits of supernatural obedience and the joys of detachment:

> The souls who truly love God cannot live without continually renouncing their own selves, their intelligence, their free will, to become ever more inflamed with this true love that seeks not sweet sensations but that desires, with ever-ready willingness, everywhere and in all things, to carry out only, simply, and exclusively the will of God, as seen through the eyes of faith, and which they love more than their own life.

And again: "He who lacks vigilance, who neglects to struggle with himself in even the least important things by incessant prayer, loses, little by little, the splendid light of faith, which through total obedience reveals the will of God . . . and he will see no more in his superiors than the pagans see in them, more or less wise and good men." He comes back time and again to this theme. Fearing that he has failed to convince them, he concludes one of his exhortations with the frightened onomatopoeia: "If anyone came to believe (but I prefer not to think of the possibility) that my observations on holy obedience are exaggerated . . . but it is better not to think of such a thing. Brrr."

All these hymns to submission did not prevent an accusing public from reproaching Kolbe for his "independent" character. It is true that renunciation pushed to this degree results in a sort of autonomy that appears to go against the rule. And then there are many superiors who are more disturbed than flattered to be considered the only qualified interpreters of the divine will and are tempted to hush up and to let the follower of "holy obedience" go his own way, thus giving him no one to obey. It is at a turning in the path of one of these long letters that we hear for the second time, like a virtuosic violin passage suddenly isolated in a rest in the score, the revealing little phrase we have heard once before: consecration to Mary should exclude all reserve, "in a word, no limits, when it happens that, for love of the Immaculate, one must die of hunger and poverty in a ditch".

And Kolbe had remained the same modest young man he had been in the seminary, when he was so afraid of the Roman women. "Ah! one other thing: on the two medals attached, which come, I believe, from Poland, one sees in an exaggerated way a leg through the dress. It's disgraceful! I feel that there is good reason to protest, so that such medals will no longer be made."

Everyone did not follow Kolbe with the same enthusiasm. He had reason to complain about his closest associate, Father Methodius. He was a "good man, and pious" but he had difficulty rising above the Conventual routine. In truth, Father Methodius did not even try to plant in his life the seed of heroism, which formed the daily bread of his brothers. He groomed his beautiful big beard, and he had one of the wicker armchairs, reserved for guests, brought into his cell. He sat there, propped against a cushion, while the other religious "had nowhere to sit but on nasty wooden stools". This relative sybaritism left Kolbe more flabbergasted than indignant. One does not go to heaven in an armchair; however, there was nothing in the rule or the constitutions to forbid it. One senses that Kolbe was disarmed by the placidity of this religious who was not disposed to getting all worked up and following a man who signed some of his letters "Mary's half-fool". Moreover, he had heard that Franciscanism was practiced in all its rigor among the Capuchins and the Friars Minor, the two other branches of the order, and not among the Conventuals, precisely the branch that he had joined. In the end they parted company.

17

India

Kolbe's enterprise was doing well; in any case, better than its founder. The Japanese doctors were horrified by his chest X rays. He had frequent attacks of fever, accompanied by trembling that shook his whole body, and in the evening he often heard the muted stampede of a migraine overtaking him. In a testimony written in Japanese and translated into Latin—one of the official languages of the canonization, the other two being French and Italian—the first doctor who examined him in Nagasaki described him as being of great sensibility, quick to react, highly nervous, but controlled. When he was counseled to go into a sanitarium, he refused. He knew that he would never be well, and he preferred to use the time left to him for work. Nevertheless he wrote to the brothers at Niepokalanow: "I am afraid to suffer. . . . But even Jesus himself, at Gethsemane, was afraid, and that thought comforts me."

Sometimes at night Kolbe was short of breath, his heart grew weaker and weaker, and he felt as if he would die right there on his pallet, holding the hand of a brother but far from his dear Poland. And when the sun rose on another day and revived him, he would simply say: "Mary has not yet called me home."

But for all that the spirit of conquest never left Kolbe. Any means was valid to inflame hearts with the love of God, "the printed word, radio broadcasts, even television [this was 1931 and television was, as yet, a baby in pajamas, with twinkling stripes], and the cinema", because "there should spring forth a Niepokalanow in every land on earth, so as to enable Mary to act by any means, even the most modern. Every technical invention, in principle, should be at her disposal." And since his illness left him respites of a month or two without fever or trembling, he took advantage of these to carry out his program. He accomplished much.

> It is a Saturday in May. "Kyuko", a direct train, is taking me to Kobe, where I will arrive tomorrow. Why? To get myself a visa and a ticket for . . . India. And why am I going there? . . . It may be possible to found another Niepokalanow there. . . . What serenity Mary's holy name brings! Let us repeat it ceaselessly from the depth of our souls, so that it becomes the breath of our hearts.

If Kolbe succeeded, there would be three Niepokalanows: one in Poland, the second in Japan, the third in India—not forgetting the fourth: in heaven, he said, with the deceased brothers.

Drifting toward Hong Kong, he wrote a great deal, dating some of his letters poetically: "At sea, such and such a day", of "in view of China's leaden mountains, on the waves of the ocean". As always, he attracted others: "I cannot manage to follow my train of thought, because a nice little pagan, who took a liking to me at the beginning of the trip, is sitting next to me, waiting for me to finish writing." With

Kolbe, there was that constant combining of global projects and extreme attention to the needs of his neighbor, especially the humble and the little. The affectionate young pagan was a soul to be baptized. It was not saltwater that he lacked. For Kolbe, the ocean probably seemed to be a vast baptismal font.

The stopover at Hong Kong was in the midst of a drought. The residents were lined up at the fountains, which gave water grudgingly and only at unforeseen times. Kolbe, thirsty and with his chest on fire, went into town to say Mass and to pray for rain, which finally fell. A passing Pole gifted him with candies, which he gave to the children. That evening he boarded a junk to return to his ship, which was hotter than ever as the rain had turned to mist. He had been impressed by the multitudes in China. "Pray", he wrote, "that I do not become a pagan among so many pagans." The risk was not great.

Between Hong Kong and Singapore, all of the passengers—mostly families of immigrants—were entirely occupied with looking for any breeze. The children, mischievous and rowdy, filled the steerage with their racket, and when finally they fell asleep, it was on the floor, side by side. When Kolbe arose, as usual before everyone else, and had to cross the darkened space to go to say his daily Mass in the salon, he had to walk very carefully so as not to step on a little hand or face. At daybreak he saw sea snakes whose color amazed him and a flight of flying fish that left behind them on the deck a long trail of small white eggs. He dreamt of Niepokalanow in Poland, of the one in Japan, and he wanted to "tear open the veil of the future", to see what the one in India would be. He passed from hope to doubt, and from fear to confidence, before finally resolving all these contradictions in faith. He was not, as I have read, a man with "a will of iron" and "nerves of steel". This metallurgy did not enter into his makeup. He was emotional, spontaneous, subject to anxiety. He sent two letters, one to Niepokalanow in Poland, another to Japan. They are so similar in every detail that they seem to be carbon copies of each other. They express this agonizing thought: "What if Niepokalanow had just collapsed?" This was a return to his usual line of reasoning, unstoppable as fatalism, but a passionate fatalism that did not end in indifference. If our work crumbles, he said, it is because Mary has decided to put an end to it, and all our efforts will be useless. If, on the contrary, she wishes us to pursue our task, we must fear nothing, not obstacles or hindrances or even "our own imperfections". His plan would succeed.

At Singapore Kolbe permitted himself, for once, an hour of sightseeing and relaxed amusement. "It seems that there are still tigers around here, not in town, however. Yesterday my good hosts took me for a walk in the vicinity, but we did not see any of these great beasts between the palms, in the rubber trees, or in the undergrowth, which is always green here—just the little monkeys at the zoological garden who greeted us as we passed."

Kolbe noted again that some of the missionaries already there were so attached to their places that they took no pleasure in the arrival of reinforcements who would oblige them to share these places. He suspected them of spending more time seeking the dollars they needed than seeking the souls who needed them. So he weighed anchor.

There Kolbe was again at sea, his thoughts floating. Off Malacca, "where sometimes one sees dark mountains on the horizon, and sometimes strips of earth just above the waves", he wrote to his Provincial, wondering: "What good is this prattling, devoid of sense or conclusion? . . . I do not know what awaits me or how to do what is to be done, and sometimes I would very much like to foresee the future." But his Provincial had recommended that he "scribble away without fear", so scribble he did while waiting to debark at Ernakulam on the west coast of India. He stayed there five days, and on the sixth he sent the following telegram to his brothers in Poland: "Inform Father Provincial: Amalam, the Indian Niepokalanow, has been founded. Glory to the Immaculata. Maximilian."

How had he been able, in less than a week, to create, or in any case obtain the means to create, a religious house, thousands of miles from the order's base, in a country he did not know? He tells how on the way back in a long letter to the Provincial, who appreciated his scribbling.

On the boat, just before debarking in India, Kolbe had met a young priest of the Syrian Catholic rite, who upon their arrival had taken him to his Bishop. The Bishop offered Kolbe generous hospitality but did not encourage him regarding his projects. A group of secular priests already had a press and printed magazines. Kolbe spent his first day studying their methods, and the battlefield. He learned that the Latin rite archbishop was not a native, which gave him some hope, and that he was a Carmelite, which diminished the hope somewhat. A foreign Archbishop should understand another foreigner better, but Kolbe was not sure that a Spanish Carmelite would understand a Polish Franciscan trained in Rome.

The next day, the archbishop's colleagues, when consulted by Kolbe about the chances of convincing His Excellency, evasively told him that he could always try. That afternoon the Syrian Bishop's car drove him to a wide river, which he crossed by boat. The Latin Archbishop was supposed to pass that way. He did indeed arrive and greeted Kolbe cordially. During the crossing, right up to the landing, he regaled Kolbe with three centuries of diocesan history in detail and left him with an invitation to lunch. Apparently Kolbe had not been able to get in a word. At this point he was, as they say in Italian, in the dark, and in French, in a fog.

The following day, as Kolbe was waiting in the hallway for the Syrian Bishop who was taking him to the Latin Archbishop, he noticed a statue of Saint Thérèse of the Child Jesus on a console. It was decorated with flowers that "looked like roses". He confided his concerns to her, according to a pact previously made with her, that stipulated that she take an interest in his mission in return for a daily prayer for her canonization. "We'll see", he said to her from the depths of his confusion, "if you remember." At that very moment, he recounted, "a flower fell onto the console. I admit that it made quite an impression on me, and I thought: 'We'll know soon enough if this is of any significance.' "

It was indeed, for the Latin Archbishop, the Spanish Carmelite who the day before had talked so much about the past just to avoid discussing the future with the unexpected and restless missionary, had completely changed his attitude. He offered Kolbe land, a house, and a chapel, and when his stupefied listener expressed concern about the conditions, His Excellency replied: "It is a gift." You have to know how to pray.

18

End of Mission

Thérèse of Lisieux, who died at age twenty-four in 1897, is without any doubt the most popular saint in the world. Contrary to the impression given by the multitude of sugary statues of her, this young girl was a great mystical genius, and her writings reach heights that show the difference between style and talent. As we have seen, Kolbe had been devoted to her since his youth, long before she was declared "Patroness of the Missions". These two spirits had to meet: they had in common the ardent desire to convert the earth, not by trying to impose any doctrine on men but by winning them to love, by love. Kolbe was not an obtuse fanatic who intended to bend others to his point of view. He believed—and he wrote—that there was in all belief outside of Catholicism some truth that one must at all costs discover so as to be able to use it as a basis for dialogue. He always sought out that bit of truth, even in Marxism, which was the exact opposite of his own belief. The young Carmelite from Lisieux also wished with all her heart that the whole world would come back to Christ. She tried to obtain this grace by the sacrifice of her own self through the slow crucifixion that is the contemplative life. Kolbe endeavored to conquer by the deployment of his creative imagination, which carried him ceaselessly through space and time far ahead of his weakened body.

On the boat that brought him back to Japan, Kolbe recalled the signs that the little sister of the Child Jesus had lavished on him. There had been the church dedicated to her, served by one of her relatives, where he had been taken on the eve of his departure from Kobe. The statues of the saint he had "bumped into", as he put it, all along the way on his journey, the episode of the rose, and the abrupt about-face by the Archbishop of Ernakulam, a Carmelite like Thérèse herself, all this seemed to him to bode well for the future of the Indian Niepokalanow. Alas! Complications, unforeseen events, and illness would prevent him from returning to India, and the rose, or "the flower that looked like a rose", that had fallen from Saint Thérèse's bouquet would wilt on the Archbishop's console, until the day when other Franciscans would come to revive it. It will, doubtless, happen. Several other Kolbe projects, such as the American and English houses, have come to fruition sooner or later after his death.

However, the Japanese climate did not suit Maximilian. Everyone noticed but he. "I have just learned", he wrote to the Father Provincial at Lvov,

> that Father Costanzo has reported to you that my health is poor. Well, I can assure you that I feel even better than I did when I left for India. To tell the truth, after the return trip, as I had been able to sleep only on the lounge chair on the deck, I have allowed myself several good nights' sleep and a midmorning snack. A swollen foot made me limp for a while, but it has gotten better without the help of medicine. I

> work as usual, on one of the refectory tables. What more can one expect? . . . These alarms raised about my health are only the result of Father Costanzo's neurasthenia. . . . He understands nothing about the ideal of Niepokalanow; he imagines that since the proclamation of the dogma, the cause of the Immaculate Conception is taken care of and that henceforth we need only honor it with a first-class celebration and a few hymns.

Like all frontline soldiers, Kolbe had trouble with rearguard mentality, which provoked a reaction rarely encountered in him: irony.

If "the good Father Costanzo" resolutely remained just short of the ideal of Niepokalanow, the others sometimes thought they could arrive at it by shortcuts. Kolbe wrote,

> These days we are learning of the problems that the Catholic schools are going through, because they do not join in the pagan rites. [At this time the Japanese paid homage to the Emperor as a sort of divinity, and the Catholics, of course, could not take part in this.] Talk of persecution has begun to spread. When the brothers heard this, their enthusiasm was such that I had to calm them by saying: "Don't rejoice too soon!" They were already imagining themselves martyrs.

The worst does not always happen. When the Japanese finally recognized Catholicism officially in 1941 they contented themselves with a simple attestation of respect for the person of the Emperor and the imperial functions. When the opportunity for supreme witness passes you by, there is always the opportunity for everyday witness, which is not always as easy to give. One thinks that one is marching toward the "ideal of Niepokalanow", the swollen foot going faster than the other, and then one realizes, all of a sudden, that one is not as detached from oneself as one would like to be:

My dear children:

While I was writing a few letters in Japanese, my pride made me believe that I am somehow capable of expressing myself in this language.

But I immediately felt that my bond of love toward the Immaculate had cooled down. I am now sitting in front of her little statue and it seems to me that she wants to reproach me and that she is angry!

My beloved children, if you ever have this feeling do not pay any attention to it. Whenever you feel guilty, even if it is because you have consciously committed a sin, a serious sin, something you have kept doing many, many times, *never let the devil deceive you by allowing him to discourage you.* Whenever you feel guilty, offer all your guilt to the Immaculate, without analyzing or examining it, as something that belongs to her. . . .

My beloved, may every fall, even if it is serious and habitual sin, always become for us a small step toward a higher degree of perfection.

In fact, the only reason why the Immaculate permits us to fall is to cure us from our self-conceit, from our pride, to make us humble and thus make us docile to the divine graces.

The devil, instead, tries to inject in us discouragement and internal depression in those circumstances, which is, in fact, nothing else than our pride surfacing again.

If we knew the depth of our poverty, we would not be at all surprised by our falls, but rather astonished, and we would thank God, after sinning, for not allowing us to fall even deeper and still more frequently. In fact, there is truly no sin deadly enough we could not fall into, were it not for the merciful hand of the Immaculate that sustains us.

We should even prefer not to experience that permanent

> sweetness our devotion for the Immaculate brings us, because that would be spiritual greed.[1]

Kolbe kept an eye on everything—a pen, too. He tempered the zeal of those aspiring to martyrdom with a phrase the turn of which drew attention. It seems to dissuade and then to promise: "Do not rejoice too soon!" He bridles the propensity of the editors of *The Knight* to emphasize: "In your thanks, don't use the words 'miracle' and 'miraculous' all over the place; the facts speak for themselves." A young monk, who doubtless thought he was imitating a Holy Fool in signing himself "Mary's dog", was advised to find another metaphor. There was nothing fanatical about Kolbe, for it is the rejection of others and their differences that makes a fanatic, and it was precisely these differences that interested him. There was nothing wild about him, because like all true mystics he distrusted those moments of disturbed sublimation where absences are taken for presences and delirium for ecstasy. He knew that he was not perfect, and his letters often resembled confessions. Indeed, he blames himself with moderation, not falling into the fault of saints from times gone by who beat their breasts, confessing so loudly to being "the greatest sinner in the world" that their guardian angel had to give them a friendly tap on the shoulder to recall them to modesty. But he loved, and that love sometimes inspired him to write, forgetting to avoid being eloquent. "My dear children, I wish for you to be nourished by the milk of Mary's graces and tenderness, to be raised by her as she raised Jesus, our older Brother, so that more and more he will recognize in us the features of the face his Mother gave him."

In 1933, Kolbe again spent several weeks in Poland, where

[1]Maximilian Kolbe, *Stronger Than Hatred: A Collection of Spiritual Writings* (New York: New City Press, 1988), pp. 104–5.

the Provincial Chapter was taking place. This solemn reunion took up little space in his correspondence. However, he is verbose about an unexpected conversion, that of a Japanese plenipotentiary minister posted to Warsaw. It seemed as if Kolbe had only left Japan to go to baptize, at the moment of his death, this son of the Rising Sun, whose wife was already Catholic.

> On the appointed day, an automobile, carrying the minister's wife, his mother, and me, drove us very rapidly to Otwock (where pulmonary illnesses are treated). On the way, I learned that the minister was pagan but that nevertheless he had permitted his children to be baptized, that he maintained good relations with the Jesuit Fathers, and that he was well disposed toward religion.
>
> That's how it happened that I visited him, and we had a little conversation on the subject of religion. He easily understood that there is only one truth, and, in consequence, there can be only one true religion. He acknowledged the existence of one God, but when we came to the mystery of the Blessed Trinity, then he observed that the Chinese have a similar belief. I acknowledged willingly that many truths, more or less deformed and muddled, are found in the world's most disparate religions.
>
> His wife gave him one of the Miraculous Medals that I had given her earlier for the family. He accepted it and put it on his nightstand.
>
> He then showed me a book in French entitled *Jesus Christ,* telling me that neither this nor a brief stay in Lourdes had convinced him.
>
> His illness was visibly far advanced and was now leading him to the tomb, as his emaciated face and translucent hands clearly indicated.
>
> During the return trip, we fixed on the Assumption as the date for the baptism of a maid who wanted to be baptized but who first needed to receive instruction.

However, we had to postpone the ceremony. On the eve of the Assumption, indeed, the minister's condition had worsened so much that we rushed to his bedside. We left the legation with the chargé d'affaires, the Japanese doctor Misawa, who had come from Berlin, and Doctor Rudzki from Warsaw. I asked Doctor Rudzki to tell me frankly, after the visit, his opinion of the patient's condition, because it was a matter of baptism.

At Otwock, Doctor Rudzki's reply was the following: "Father, what you have to do, do it right away; the patient will die today."

Meanwhile the Apostolic Nuncio had been informed. Something had urged him to return from vacation before the Assumption and not afterward as he had planned. I had been able to reach him by telephone, and he had promised to come as soon as possible. We had decided to wait for him. As soon as he appeared in the corridor I informed him of the situation, and he went to the patient. He reminded him of their old friendship and presented the fundamental truths of the Faith.

During this time, on the other side of the door, the minister's wife, his sister, two priests, secretaries to the Nuncio, and myself all prayed silently for the sick man, each for his own reasons.

And the grace of faith descended on the noble heart of the minister. After several enlightenments, he responded to an explicit question from the Nuncio: "I believe, I believe." "And you wish to be baptized?" "I wish it."

The Nuncio poured the water over his head, saying: "Francis, I baptize you in the name of the Father, of the Son, and of the Holy Spirit."

After the baptism, as those around him can testify, a great joy entered the minister's heart. Several hours later his soul, pure as an angel, was welcomed by the Immaculata into paradise, on the eve of her Assumption.

In the minister's house, those among his relatives and his

servants who had not yet been baptized were baptized three weeks later. I have quoted this letter nearly in its entirety for the simple reason that it is much longer than the others, and it shows to what point Kolbe was attentive to people, who were in his eyes infinitely more important than events. One could say that it was, in this case, "a plenipotentiary minister", a personage of sufficient importance to prompt the deployment of an apostolic nuncio, two doctors, and three priests; but it was not so much the diplomat who interested Maximilian Kolbe; it was the Japanese man.

On his return to Nagasaki, Kolbe wrote nicely to his mother: "The trip went well. We were not drowned, contrary to what the brothers at Niepokalanow feared upon learning of the sinking of the Japanese boat." His mother was reassured about her son, but Kolbe was not reassured about his mother. We do not know what sort of wish she had expressed on the occasion of some exchange of greetings that moved her son to deem it necessary to tell her: "It really isn't that easy to die." In spite of her undeniable religious vocation, perhaps she was finding it difficult, since the death of Joseph, to bear Maximilian's being so far away and the disappearing of her eldest son, Francis, of whom they had no news. Perhaps she had expressed, in disquieting terms, how tired she was of being so often and so cruelly separated from those she loved. Kolbe hoped to restore her courage a little by adding, after his remark on the difficulty of dying: "There will be another Provincial Chapter in two years; I will come once again to knock at the door in Smolensk Street." That was the address of Maria Kolbe's convent. Two years—that seemed to him a reasonable time span between two visits of a personal nature, which had no direct bearing on the conversion of the planet.

Kolbe had not drowned, but he risked being submerged by work. As a journalist, he swam in ink and tirelessly blackened paper with his publications, which came out of one another like Russian dolls. As a spiritual director, he instructed the novices, trained the seminarians, and counseled the brothers, who sometimes knew nothing, and the priests, who did not know everything. Founder, he defined the strategy and tactics of his mission, all the while observing, out of the corner of his eye, the other orders established in Japan, who saw him more as a competitor than as an ally. There was also the bishop of the area, whose goodwill had to be maintained by a few demonstrations of courtesy. He exhorted, he encouraged, watching from afar over the Polish Niepokalanow, reporting to his superiors with great punctuality, for he preached fluently a theology of obedience, and some of these men, it will be remembered, had already thought of recalling the expedition. And he prayed, that prayer that became luminous as it rose, and for him tended more and more to be condensed in a single word: "Mary". Mary, who bloomed in all his letters and summed up his thought. Mary, "so close to the Blessed Trinity", "profound mystery" who only "a presumptuous mind, and moreover a stupid one", would have the impertinence to explain. There are things, he said, "that can only be learned kneeling". And: attachment to Mary "is not a matter of intelligence or of sentiment but of will".

There are, all the same, graces, personal revelations that the Devil's Advocate distrusted as much as apparitions. He seemed to discern in the Servant of God (he refers to Kolbe, the accused) a tendency to let himself be guided by private revelations rather than to remain "solidly anchored in the truths taught by the Church". The prosecution speaks: "Thus, he had been assured of his eternal salvation by a promise supposedly received from the Most Blessed Virgin." Indeed, Kolbe declared solemnly one day to his brothers: "I have been assured of my heaven, in all certainty." But, as it is only by divine revelation that we can know that our sins have been forgiven, it is important to know in what way this promise had been made to him. The record of the investigation does not state it clearly. On the contrary, the facts are reported in a manner that makes one think that Father Kolbe believed in a dream. Father Florians Kocura tells it thus: "I heard it recounted by the other brothers that the servant of God, during his stay in Japan, *and during his serious illness,* had had an apparition of the Virgin Mary, who had guaranteed that he would be saved." The Devil's Advocate underlined the words "and during his serious illness". Fever can lead to delirium.

Kolbe's health was poor, even though he pretended to laugh about it: "It seems that some people think I already have one foot in the other world. One foot perhaps, but not the right hand, which is writing to you, or the left hand, which is holding the paper." He made no fuss at all when the order set a superior over him who was charged with relieving him of some of his innumerable tasks and softening the in some sense heroic regimen of the foundation where the Franciscan cord was at its tightest. There would be a rest at noon, recreation in the evening, and, above all, an exquisite memory of home; they would eat pigs' feet, Polish style, which cheered up the whole group, even Kolbe. He took advantage of all this to take on yet another care: starting a daily in Poland, the *Maly Dziennik* (the *Little Journal*), which started on the road to success following the way of all the other publications in what must now be called his group.

"I know very well", Kolbe wrote to his Provincial, "that objections will begin to rain down from a good thousand theoreticians. But as soon as the print run has surpassed that of the other dailies and reached almost one hundred twenty thousand copies, the objections will lose their force, that is, if they don't stop altogether." In this world there is always a "but". From afar, he sent directives across Siberia. They had to begin with a little newspaper, a small format, modest in every respect, for a one-month trial only. If the experiment was conclusive, they would continue. They would register the newspaper with several press agencies until they had their own. As there were Franciscans everywhere, they would not lack correspondents. The paper would thus give the latest news, and since the purpose was to send Mary into the greatest possible number of homes, the price would be very low, about the equivalent of the two-penny prewar paper. Distribution? Newsboys, who in the big cities could be members of the Militia, would be paid from sales. "The boys who traverse the cities from end to end must be able to live from their work, and perhaps they will learn at the same time." This paper was to be *The Knight* and the daily news, along with moral and spiritual commentaries. The editorial costs would be nil, the distribution little and the machines being amortized by *The Knight;* the expense would be reduced to ink and paper: they could meet all competition.

Number zero, a sort of pasteup of the future daily, arrived from Niepokalanow in Poland in December 1934, with a request for Kolbe's critique. He delivered it immediately.

As to the price: Kolbe recommended that it be higher than foreseen, say, five cents instead of two, realizing, however, that there were not many coins of the five-cent denomination in circulation.

Regarding the title: Kolbe said that it "falls" well (a typographic expression).

About the layout: Kolbe felt that it showed the effect of

excessive haste. There were lines and in some cases columns in a wayward state.

In the first issue, the staff set forth their intentions in grandiose terms under the heading "What we want", which resembled American propaganda during the Second World War: "Why we fight". "So that our daily may fight with dignity for the honor of Catholicism", wrote the future editor-in-chief, Father Marian, it should have a rich and varied content, a splendid and artistic typographic presentation, and be in every respect worthy of its sublime content. The cards of introduction to the critics were not distinguished by their humility. Kolbe did not share the point of view of the editor-in-chief: "I do not feel that it is advisable to worry about changing the content and presentation to render them worthy of a Catholic daily; it is proper rather to leave it modest and at a price that favors a large circulation among the people." He adds with gentle irony that we may reach the heights where dwells "the dignity of Catholic organs of the press".

Along the same lines and still alluding to the issue of presentation: "To insist on the fact that lack of belief spreads from educated people to uneducated ones could introduce the idea that science estranges one from faith, which is not the truth."

Regarding the Jews, the editor had, it seems, shown a touch of anti-Semitism. It should be a question not of excluding the Jews from commerce but rather of "contributing to the growth of Polish businesses". Kolbe had already explained repeatedly to his companions that the Jews were, above all else, souls to be won, like any others, by love. It seems that some of them had been more or less influenced by public opinion, which reproached the Jews for being different after having compelled them to remain so—the vicious circle of minorities whose acceptance is delayed. Kolbe did not go along with this thinking.

As for the rest, Kolbe approved—most of all, of course, the publisher's name "Presses of the Immaculata". That is very beautiful, he said, and correct, because the enterprise is hers. Or should be. He would not always be in agreement with the spirit of the *Little Journal,* as we shall see. It was published from May 27, 1935, until September 4, 1939, the beginning of the rapid suppression of Poland by the concerted operations of Hitler's army and the Soviet forces. One million copies of the last issue were printed.

Kolbe was interested not only in his newspapers and his apostolate. He was also concerned about the health of his companions. About Brother Alexis, who was in the midst of an acute crisis of scrupulosity such as he himself had suffered at the same age and which he thus understood better than anyone else. About Brother Yves, weighed down by pain, which did not, though, keep him from smiling and joking and whose courage Kolbe admired. But while Father Maximilian was observing the suffering of others, the new superior at Nagasaki was observing him and sharing his anxieties with the community at Niepokalanow in Poland.

> Father Maximilian is ill. He coughs and speaks of fatigue. He just went to the doctor. I am afraid for him.... The Immaculata knows what difficulties we have fallen into with the school, the seminary, *The Knight*.... Pray! That we can at least lead the seminarians to their priestly ordination.... Since last summer, Father Maximilian has grown weaker and weaker.

Moreover, and in spite of his indifference toward himself, Kolbe knew where he stood. In May 1935 he wrote: "Most Reverend Father Procurator General, would you do something to please me? I feel rather worn out, and I do not know when my earthly pilgrimage may finish.... But I would be happy if, before closing my eyes, I could see—if it pleases Mary—the Militia's official act of consecration to the Immaculata." He really wanted to see the entire Franciscan order consecrated to Mary by an additional vow. The idea was well received, but it had to be passed on by the hierarchy, the theologians, and the lawyers, which was a rather complicated process for a simple idea.

In a very long letter written July 12, 1935, to a priest at Niepokalanow, Kolbe spoke indirectly of the pains he was suffering, which for him were a part of the logical order of spiritual combat.

> There is no birth without pain. Besides, could there be any sacrifices too great, where Mary is concerned? We have consecrated ourselves to her not only in theory but also, quite really, in practice. And if we do not tire of struggling to conquer the world for her, sufferings will not cease to fall upon us, and the more valiantly we fight, the heavier and more numerous they will be. But only until death. Afterward, there will be the resurrection. And even if (but that would be impossible) Mary would never reward us, we would nonetheless consecrate ourselves to her with fervor and enthusiasm, for it is not the recompense but her whom we love.

Kolbe's physical ruin only sharpened his mind, which became even more brotherly. Though he had a hard time holding a pen, he furnished ten pages of mystical theology to a good Father who did not know how to divide his heart between his different devotions, or ten pages of practical wisdom to the brothers at Niepokalanow. They seemed consumed by a building fever. "Your projects for solid construction worry me", he told them. "Will Niepokalanow slip slowly toward the mediocrity of permanent buildings? The edifices with which you plan to replace your barracks will be less easy to adapt to new needs, to say nothing of the fact that in case of political upheaval they would be attractive for requisition. What you will spend on buildings would be better reserved for the propagation of the Faith." "Have you forgotten that our first treasurer was Blessed Joseph Cottolengo, glued in the cardboard box where we deposited the first pennies given to the cause so dear to us? I am sending you a picture of him." One never knows. He complained about only one thing, the lack of time, which prevented him from responding as he would have liked to the confidence of "the pagans" who turned to him in ever greater numbers and whose "proverbial hardness" was beginning to melt.

Today, Japan is one of the world's great powers, and it seems capable of setting its cohesion and determination victoriously against any challenge in history. But the atomic bomb not only ravaged two of its cities; it also attacked Japan in its ancient beliefs. One discerns an imperceptible crack that exposes it to brutal collective depression like a sudden earthquake. Should that happen, perhaps Japan would remember the little Franciscan with the great beard who loved "the people with almond eyes" and whose monastery at Nagasaki opened its doors to the first orphans of the nuclear era. A people should not live long without faith.

However, the pigs' feet were not the answer to everything, and it had become necessary to snatch Kolbe from the climate that was destroying him and take him back to Poland. The superior, who was gently watching over him, was not about to let the occasion pass by; he sent him to the new Provincial Chapter. In March 1936 Kolbe announced his departure to his mother. "If the war does not unleash its storm, I will leave here for Poland the beginning of June if we are to travel by sea, or at the end of the month if we can cross Siberia." It would be sooner.

On May 25 he wrote to the brothers at Nagasaki: "While the ship was carrying me farther and farther from the shore, this thought came to me: What if I am looking at this land for the last time? And something made my eyes grow moist."

It was indeed the last time.

19

The Monsters

The absence of eternal laws leads to barbarism. The French revolutionaries had understood that; they promulgated their Declaration of the Rights of Man and of the Citizen under the now-forgotten preamble "in the presence and under the auspices of the Supreme Being". It did not speak of God—that would have recalled the old order—but they knew that without a divine security, without a "Supreme Being" who could sanctify the principles of law, there was no rein on the ruling power or on the law, which could impose itself on consciences. At the same time it would be a rule and a protection for the individual. One is not obliged to acknowledge this truth, one is not obliged to believe it, but one is obliged to live it. The Europe of reason, so proud of having vanquished the Europe of faith and no longer even honoring the Supreme Being with a courtesy reference, was about to learn from experience as the gentle folly of the 1920s turned to the furious madness of the 1930s. The rights of man would be abolished by the monsters of the totalitarian brood. Class hatred, racial hatred, hate for the Jews, hate for the "bourgeois democracy"—hate became, for the first time in the world, a fundamental principle of human societies. It was the great innovation of the century.

To the east, the system engendered by political hatred forbade man all other finality but himself and, in consequence, enclosed and padlocked the circles of his own purgatory. The party formed itself into an idol—for it is appropriate here to speak not of ideology but of idolatry. It demanded submission, punished skepticism, and from 1933 onward, after the great trials in Moscow, began to take or to shoot its own high priests. Every religion needs a Judas, and Judases come from the ranks of the disciples. In Italy, fascism adopted black, the color of anarchy and widowhood, to indicate the extinction of all laws in favor of the arbitrary, putting recalcitrants under the threat of immediate widowhood. In Germany, the hoarse voice that sounded like the crackling of the hunting horn brought a mythology out of the forest. This mythology of race and blood was of an Aryan people chosen by nature, which had made them beautiful, blond, muscular, predestined for victory and domination. Their leader was physically just the opposite—these things do happen—Hitler was small, dark, a little fat, and walked like a duck. The people chosen by nature would naturally be the enemies of the people chosen by God, whose essential characteristic, the cause of the persecutions they had undergone for centuries, was that they were without idols. This new paganism would end by requiring human sacrifices. The classic Aryan who idolized himself and who existed only in his own dreams could not bear to see the Jew, evidence of divine reality, and he would kill him.

In 1936, the same year when Kolbe returned to Poland, Spain was bloodied by a hard-fought military coup d'état. The revolutionary legions waged their civil war like a sort of interior crusade against the infidels. The republicans fought to the point that in their vocabulary they called hope and that was really growing despair; they had on their side the law, a few rifles, and the frightened sympathy of Western democracies, which discreetly looked away at the moment of the kill.

England, wrapped in its fogs, sipped the last revenues from its empire and sought compromises with the devil. They were to sign a naval agreement with Hitler that would preserve their mastery of the sea by risking the loss of the mastery of their destiny. Waiting for the day when they would be solitary and sublime, they prepared to confide power to one of their most distinguished sons. Neville Chamberlain, who would give his name to an umbrella, gave it to a policy. In France the Popular Front endeavored to make up for the incredible backwardness of a "land of liberty" where there existed only two social laws. The one, from 1848, forbade the employment in mines of children under twelve years of age. The other, from 1793, prohibited "coalitions", in other words, trade unions. Unfortunately, they would accomplish this necessary task under cover of a simplified metaphysics in which war is the deed of capitalists and arms dealers, to the point that they would not know how to wage war when the capitalists and arms dealers were excluded from power. This slapdash optimism rendered the government hard of hearing and somewhat deaf to the sound of the boots that shook the earth on the other side of the border. All the same, on March 7, 1936, the blond Aryans, under the command of the little dark-haired man, had, without encountering any opposition, achieved a military occupation of the left bank of the Rhine. France tolerated this violation of its treaties with little emotion. It had total confidence in the concrete of the Maginot Line, which would never stop any army but the French.

Caught between two totalitarian powers that would come into contact by passing over its body, Poland, not without cold sweat, relied on its alliances with the victors of the First World War. But it was well aware that the setting for the next apocalypse was being erected around it. With his country threatened, Maximilian Kolbe felt again the instincts and automatic tendencies toward covert action he had known in his youth, when he had discreetly crossed the interior borders of his country, murderously occupied by the Prussians, the Russians, and the Austrians. For that reason his newspapers made no allusion to the events, and also for another reason, expressed in a letter written from Nagasaki to the community at the Polish Niepokalanow: "The editors and contributors must be required to write according to the spirit of the Marian Militia, that is, the conquest of the world for the Immaculata, the salvation and the sanctification of souls, avoiding, when it is not absolutely necessary, criticism of men, parties, and other nations." This was the directive of a purely religious intelligence for whom evil would destroy itself before the evidence of good. This was also, in a country so often martyred, the reflex of the oppressed, who takes the surest line of resistance, that of going through the secrecy of the absolute.

20

The Return

Just off the boat from Japan, Kolbe was elected superior of the great Niepokalanow in Poland by the order's Provincial Chapter. Perhaps it was a generous way of keeping him in a climate that would be more favorable to his health. Or perhaps his presence had become necessary to an enterprise that was beginning to attain phenomenal proportions. For, in the vigilant absence of its founder, the work had not ceased to grow. On the land given by the Polish count, who had so feared displeasing the Virgin Mary, the buildings—of light materials—had been enlarged or expanded; the "editorial monastery" had become an industrial enterprise, an organized village. With its twelve departments that were veritable ministries (of production, finance, professional training, exterior relations, and so on), its warehouses of provisions and clothing, its hospital, its dentists, its radio station, its type foundry and its firemen, its workshops for mechanical assembly, its three ultramodern presses running at top speed, and its hundreds of religious who printed, worked, or invented (for example: a patented "addressograph") Niepokalanow was a power. They had celebrated their tenth anniversary in 1937, and Kolbe asked Pope Pius XI for his blessing in this report of their activities.

> The Marian Militia today numbers nearly a million members. The national center of the Militia, first established at Cracow, then at Grodno, was moved in 1927 to a new monastery near Warsaw, called Niepokalanow. There are now six hundred religious there and twenty-seven seminarians.
>
> This monastery publishes (1) the monthly magazine of the movement, intended for adults, *The Knight of the Immaculata,* circulation 780,000; (2) a second magazine, for young people, *The Little Knight,* circulation 180,000; (3) a daily, *The Little Journal,* circulation 130,000,

to which eight other periodicals would be added. One may wonder if this letter, piously conserved in the archives of the order and not in those of the Vatican, was ever sent. In any case, the blessing did not come.

Like all powers, Niepokalanow had its enemies. Some antireligious presses led a campaign against this odd monastery where state-of-the-art technology and asceticism joined forces to inundate the country with inexpensive publications that spoke of the supernatural in an exasperatingly natural way. Even within the Church, Niepokalanow did not have only friends. In Kolbe's correspondence one sees, passing at a distance, the mysterious figure of one "Don N. N.", never referred to otherwise, who leaves behind him a faint odor of sulphur. This person, sufficiently well placed to do some damage and who did not miss the chance to try, seems to have taken it upon himself to destroy Kolbe's work, by intrigue, infiltration, and all the means that connections and worldliness can put at the service of malevolence. That enemy faded away; others were to come, in trench coats and slouch hats, eyes empty of all recognizable sentiment, going about in twos like mismatched twins: the Gestapo. But they were not yet there.

In their joy at seeing Kolbe again, and their fear that his frailty would not withstand the snows of Poland any better than it had the damp sunshine of Japan, the tailors at Niepokalanow had given him a fur coat. He refused it. They fell back on a quilted jacket. He consented to wear that only after having observed that all the sick in the monastery had the same one. He would never agree to being treated differently than the brothers: a superior should be distinguished by only an increase in duties and an excess of responsibilities.

To Kolbe's worries a secret pain was now added: the wanderings of his brother Francis. The latter, employed at the town hall in Grodno, was living with a woman other than his wife. It would be easy to reach him, Kolbe wrote to his mother, but "if I try to do that, he will soon slip away once again, for fear that I'll try to bring him back to his first wife". This "poor Francis" was a fish who rose to any bait. If he had trouble resisting temptation, he did resist the Nazi occupation; but Maximilian, who had seen him leave the order, would not have the joy of seeing him leave his own disorder. Maximilian's heart might be affected by it, but not his serenity. The gift of one's self certainly does not shelter one from what religion used to call "crosses", but it does help one to accept them as a sort of unmerited grace. "God enters us through our wounds", a great mystic once said. Kolbe was cheerful, and a sad religious seemed to him an anomaly. What hold can melancholy have on us when we have given all? For him, many psychological sufferings resulted from an imperfect dedication. He thought, as do many spiritual people, that there is something within us that has perhaps even unconsciously distracted us from the offering of ourselves and that it is this that produces those small painful concretions of refusal that are to the soul what calculus is to the organism. This idea comes up often in his letters. He himself had held back nothing of his gifts in his personal immolation. According to Saint Paul: "All things contribute to the well-being of him who loves God." Strong in this certainty, Kolbe was invariably smiling. It took him to heaven. He even had days when his brothers, astonished, had the impression that he had not come back.

During this final period of his short life, Kolbe wrote more letters than articles. He contributed little to the daily founded in his absence. It seemed to him to be too much engaged in the political battle. Hence, the directive:

> To combat evil according to the spirit of the Marian Militia is to fight with love for all men, including those who are less good. It is to put goodness in relief, so as to make it more attractive, rather than to propagate evil by describing it. When the occasion presents itself to call the attention of society, or of authority, to some evil, it must be done with love for the person to blame, and with delicacy. Do not exaggerate; do not go into detail about the evil any more than is necessary to remedy it.

Fifty years later, we find the same attitudes in Pope John Paul II. Seated at table with him a regular visitor pointed out, without naming the authors, the extravagances of certain trendy theologies (currently being discredited). The Pope replied, with his usual calm, "Let error destroy itself."

In his articles, which do not have the infinite variety of his letters, Kolbe returns often to the same subjects. First and foremost is atheism, which seems to him to be the result of deficient logic. For him, reason can prove the existence of God, and one senses that he is ready to affirm that it has never proved anything else. Faith itself "is an act of reason, which, with the cooperation of the will and divine grace, recognizes a high truth". Before the complexity of the universe, he cries out with Voltaire, who was not really one of his friends, "I do not want to believe that this clock exists and has no clockmaker." This simplified explanation would always seem sufficient to him, and it is true that the most arrogant metaphysics, when all is said and done, goes no further: the world is, or is not, a clock.

Moreover, Kolbe published little, as great a journalist as he was; between 1936 and 1940, he wrote forty or so pieces, several of which were mere brief communiqués, good wishes, petals of thought. "In Spring all is reborn. Just so, our spirit of consecration to Mary revives." "Let us act in such a way that others will love her as we do, and even more than we do." The first of this final series of articles defined once again the ideal of Niepokalanow, of the Militia, of the *Little Journal,* to which Kolbe contributed hardly any articles. I believe that he preferred *The Knight,* whose rosary had an answer for everything and which did not let itself be swept up, like the daily, in the turbulence of the news. The *Little Journal* did not respond, it seemed to him, to the wish he had expressed at the birth of *The Knight,* namely, that he could put on his masthead "Mary, editor-in-chief", for even if he was followed and often obeyed, he was not always understood. Really, he was rarely understood. The princes of the spirit are always alone. The force of the concentration of their intelligence on a thought, when they belong to that category of exceptional beings that Carlyle called "heroes", or on a mystery, when they are religious, is such that it isolates them from even their most faithful companions, who admire them without seeing what it is they see, from the crowds who place their trust in their person rather than in understanding their ideas, and from the vague circle of intellectuals who, never able to attain the point of incandescence of those spirits who encounter an eternal and living truth, suppose that this point does not exist and hold that those who remain dazzled by it are dreamers, or sick. Solitude is the lot of the conquerors, the adventurers of thought, and the great mystics. Napoleon, with three hundred thousand men who did not know where they were going, traveled Europe alone, pursuing a transcendental and elusive unity. Socrates sought the truth so far in advance of his contemporaries that they had to put him to death to have him finally under their feet. The mystic had that characteristic of being able to say all in one word, a name, the name of a person who condenses in himself all possible thoughts, in a cohesion that is literally nuclear and renders faith at once inscrutable and fascinating.

For Saint Teresa of Avila this name that said all was that of Jesus, which she always had followed by an exclamation point, graphic symbol of ecstasy. In her ecstasies, Saint Catherine of Siena repeated unceasingly, "God, God, O holy God . . . ", and it was not, as unbelievers suppose, a sort of joker word that Christians use when they are lacking a card but the source of truth that lit everything with a new light. For Kolbe that inexhaustible and revealing word was the name of Mary, and if he uttered it at the beginning, in the middle, and at the end of all his letters and all his articles, it was because he had, each time, the impression that he was lighting a candle, a Chinese lantern, or a star, and he never tired of making garlands or milky ways. Simple hearts listened to him because holiness always finds them well disposed. The others, in their blindness, accused him of harping on.

However, with his millions of readers and his army of monks, Kolbe still gave the impression of being alone. He seemed to be always one step ahead, guided by the strange movements of a star, like one of the Three Kings and ready to leave his followers far behind to arrive sooner at the foot of a crib that inspired in him such lovely prayers:

> O Immaculata, what were your thoughts when for the first time you placed the Divine Infant on his bed of straw? What feelings inundated your heart while you wrapped him in swaddling clothes, held him to your heart, and nursed him at your breast?
>
> You knew very well who that Child was, because the prophets had spoken of him, and you understood them better than all the Pharisees and the learned Scripture scholars. The Holy Spirit had given to you infinitely more enlightenment than to all other souls together. Besides, how many of the mysteries of Jesus were revealed only and exclusively to your immaculate soul by the Divine Spirit that lived and operated in you!
>
> Already, at the moment of the Annunciation, the Most Holy Trinity, through the ministry of an angel, had presented to you, in all its clarity, its plan of redemption, and had awaited your response. At that moment you knew perfectly to whom your consent was being given and whose Mother you were to be!
>
> And there he was before you, in his newborn fragility.
>
> What feelings of humility, of love, and of gratitude must have filled your heart . . . while you marveled at the humility, the love, and the gratitude that God incarnate showed to you.
>
> I beg you to fill my heart too with your humility, your love, and your gratitude!

These lines are an extract from *L'Echo de Niepokalanow.* I wonder if there could have been any other mind to publish thoughts of this kind, in that prewar Europe, dazed by the din of voluble hatred and vain exorcism of fear, slipping toward the night.

At Niepokalanow, the troops charged along, but not everyone was able to keep up; there were a few who were lame. One of these had broken two of his vows (obedience and poverty) after having confessed, in tears, that he had difficulty with the third (chastity). Kolbe advised him to stay at home, where the unhappy boy had gone at his own expense and without permission. But Kolbe gave the advice without acrimony, recommending to the guilty party that he "cling to the Immaculata", who would doubtless be with him "to the peaceful end of his earthly life". These defections were rare. "The level of spiritual life of the brothers at Niepokalanow is good, I should even say very good", wrote Kolbe to his Provincial. "The number of 'accidents', even though there were five in one year, was still below 1 percent. It is better, thus, than among the first apostles, where the percentage was one out of twelve!" Humor, obviously. Kolbe knew very well that his comparison did not measure up; the boys who had left were not Judases; they were not going to go out and hang themselves. On the contrary, they would remain faithful to the memory of Kolbe. Some would regret from the bottom of their hearts not having been able to impose on themselves the sacrifices he made so easily—seemingly without effort—with the sober enthusiasm of ancient athletes for corporal penance. "Concerning mortifications," Kolbe said to one brother, "you must be prudent, so as not to endanger your health; for our health is not ours; it belongs to Mary." He followed this by saying that a religious is but the tenant of his consecrated person, and that it is his duty to maintain the premises in good order.

The Devil's Advocate disputed this point of view. Using a text by Pope Benedict XIV emphasizing that proof of bodily mortifications is necessary to assess the sanctity of a servant of God, he observed that "Father Kolbe's life, entirely spent in different forms of apostolic activity, showed a total absence of this essential requirement." In Kolbe's life he saw no trace of this "genuine sign of Christian perfection". He referred to the reports of the apostolic procurators. The one had no examples of extraordinary penances to quote; others confined themselves to stating that the servant of God behaved like his brothers, "except for his stays in the mountains", and that he took an hour of rest in the afternoon, on doctor's orders, following this prescription "conscientiously".

The Devil's Advocate diluted a drop of irony in this "conscientiously", sighed, and passed on to another objection. Did Father Kolbe at least compel himself to practice the penances imposed by the ancient constitutions of the order, such as the "holy exercise of the discipline", which consisted, as we know, of flagellating one's back oneself or through the obliging intervention of a fellow religious? The prosecution did not know. It noted that as superior, Kolbe should have watched over the communal application of the penances imposed by the order during Lent.

The defense, dumbfounded, began by replying, in its embarrassment, that in any case Kolbe did not smoke or drink alcohol and that he traveled third class. Then, returning to its senses, it turned Benedict XIV against the prosecution, reminding it that for this Pope "mortifications were not virtues" and that they were to be used in moderation. With his bouts of fever, his migraines, and his damaged lung, was Kolbe not already sufficiently manhandled by nature, or did he need to add a whip? As for the communal penance during Lent, the defense reported that at Niepokalanow it had been replaced, with all necessary authorizations, by the recitation of the *Miserere.* Kolbe, it was said, preferred the spirit to the letter, all the more so as seven hundred monks lashing each other with cords in their chapel would not have presented a very edifying spectacle for the novices.

Religion, as the Japanese experience has already shown us, penetrates the human being long before any philosophy. It reaches the depths where anguish gathers and from where rise the primordial questions to which ideologies and ways of thought give brief responses from the intellect when what are wanted are responses from life itself. It was in that region of the soul that Kolbe had chosen to live, and he would not be dislodged by the din of the century. It is useless to search his articles, his talks, or his letters for a direct commentary on current events; there is none. While evil blanketed the earth little by little, he worked in the spiritual gold mine, and he refused to come out and engage himself and his work in the combat on the surface. He did not want the chapel he had built turned into an ammunition depot, and that was not neutralism. He was anti-Nazi as much as he was anti-Marxist and more of a patriot than ever. Moreover, he sensed that his country would soon once again be found only in the hearts of its people. An old letter tells us more than any long treatise on the difficulty of being Polish:

> Aboard the *Ankor,* July 1932.
>
> At the post office in Ernakulam, a city on the Malabar coast of India, I wrote a telegram in Polish to send to Niepokalanow. The agent, a good Catholic, wanted to send it out promptly, but he quoted me such a price that I was flabbergasted and I protested.
>
> So he began to look through the tariffs carefully.
>
> "Polish, what language is that?" he asked.
>
> I replied: "The language the thirty-two million people in Poland speak."
>
> And he asked: "Poland is in Austria, isn't it?"

> "Poland, sir, is in Poland. It is an independent state."
>
> Again he looked at the rates. Finally, tired out, the poor fellow succeeded in finding an acceptable one.
>
> In the train from Colombo S.L. a traveler of the intellectual type asked me where I was going and from where I came.
>
> "I am Polish", I told the man. "I come from Poland."
>
> "Then", my intellectual friend replied, "you are Russian."
>
> "I had to convince him that Poland was not Russia."

In the bus someone explained to him that the Polish restaurant to which he was going was a Russian restaurant. Someone else informed him that the religion of Poland was Judaism; he knew, being himself a Jew of German origin and employed at the French consulate in Shanghai and thus well informed.

Kolbe hesitated to correct "such a good man". All the same, he did tell him that "the Polish population was composed, for the most part, of Catholics".

In 1938, Poland was not in Austria, but Austria was in Germany, where the pagan gods of force and of dream had come out of the forests, and Christianity had confined them. They promised one of the earth's culturally richest peoples that they would become pure, handsome, and healthy like their mother nature. They gave birth to a sort of microcephalic dragon covered with scales of steel, whose tongue of fire would reduce Europe to ashes. Like all the Poles, Kolbe saw clearly that this mythologic monster was beginning to turn its head toward his country. There was no help forthcoming from the Stalinist giant, apparently asleep, whose cold eye seemed already to be sizing up the dismemberment. And he said:

> My children, a merciless battle is coming. I do not know exactly what will happen, but here in Poland we should expect the worst. The war is much closer than we might

> think, and it will disperse our community. . . . When it comes, we should thank our persecutors and express our gratitude to them, so as to obtain for them the grace of conversion through Mary's intercession. As for us, we are invincible. . . .
>
> [In any case], there is no corner of the world where one does not find crosses. . . . Let us not try too hard to flee them but, if we must, take them on our shoulders and carry them willingly, for love of the Immaculata. How sweet will be the death of those who belong to her!

Sweet . . . , but according to his logic, sweetness came with a peaceful conscience.

During the years that led to the war, Kolbe's correspondence dealt with routine affairs. Major ones, such as the extension of the Marian Militia, the circulation of the press, the spirit of Niepokalanow, new foundations; minor ones such as the difficulties caused by a nice little brother returned from a cure of several months "after having gotten rid of his bacilli and absorbed such a quantity of worldliness" that he had become useless. There was the portrait of the ideal porter:

> The porter should be old enough, in age and vocation, and well rooted in the religious spirit, because he is the one who represents the community to those who come to the door of the monastery. Visitors often judge the whole community by his conduct. He should be capable of controlling himself, so that his own spirituality does not suffer from his contacts with the world. He should arm himself with patience, delicacy, affability, but sometimes he should show a firmness and keep his head in all circumstances, even when a madman—and it happens—brandishes a revolver. A single word spoken without the needed kindness can cause great damage. During the absence of the regular porter one day, a brother treated

someone brusquely only to see that he was at the head of a group of visitors who immediately retraced their steps.

Maximilian Kolbe also took charge of setting up a large radio station; the one at Niepokalanow had not yet received its authorization to broadcast except on an amateur basis. As we know, he had always been interested in modern communications technology. At age thirteen, he had already invented and done supporting drawings for a system of telegram transmission that strongly resembled a telex. But on "the sound and fury" of the world, still nothing. It must be said that, for Kolbe, unhappiness was the fall. There was one within his view, that of a companion who seemed to have reached the heights and then had broken his vows. "Let us pray for his soul. . . . There is real suffering, next to which all material disasters, sickness, and death are nothing."

After all, the Gospel, turned entirely toward people, ignored events and did not speak of Tiberias any more than Kolbe did of Hitler.

All the same, Kolbe unleashed his patriotic sentiments once, in a letter to Marshal Rydz-Smigly, the political heir of Marshal Pilsudski, written in May 1939. Hitler had already devoured Austria and Czechoslovakia. The Western democracies, which had only one thought—to elude an encounter between fear and destiny—had gone to Munich to assure the glutton of their peaceful frame of mind without daring to ask him for proof of his. In England, Winston Churchill, that incarnation of national heroism who looked like a pouting baby plunged into a too-hot bath, cried for the benefit of the surrounding cowards, "You have chosen dishonor to avoid war; you are dishonored and you will have war." It was clear that Hitler's next victim would be Poland.

"Thoroughly convinced of the need for effort and sacrifices

that the present situation imposes on all the citizens of our nation, the 619 religious of Niepokalanow and the 120 seminarians have decided to give up sugar. . . . The sum thus saved will be their contribution to the needs of the army." For this occasion, the Immaculata was named Protectress of Poland. This deprivation of sugar seems a small thing, but the religious, who possessed nothing and lived on very little, had nothing else to offer.

Kolbe's following letters return to the subject of everyday life: missionary activity, the publications, the religious professions, and the accidents, the defections, always mourned, always as cruel for the heart of a man whose soul thrilled in unison with other souls and who was torn apart by discord. There were the small treacheries of the sulphurous person we have already met, who wanted the downfall of Niepokalanow and was now emptying the mailbox at the monastery with a piece of wire. Kolbe continued his insistent reminders about Marian spirituality, or what was gently called do-it-yourself piety, such as his invitation to the musicians at Niepokalanow. The monastery had its own orchestra, and he asked them to imitate those at Zakopane, who gave the Virgin Mary trumpet voluntaries, patterned on popular melodies, as softly as these instruments of the last judgment permitted.

Even if the tone of Kolbe's letters did not change, the tone of his talks to the brothers at Niepokalanow became more and more serious and began to resemble the Gospel toward its end. The night before he was taken Jesus said to his disciples: "The hour is coming, indeed it had already come, when you will all be scattered, each going his own way, and you will leave me alone. But I am not alone, because the Father is with me."

Kolbe said: "My children, today I am with you; you love

me, and I love you. But it will not always be so: I will die, and you will live. However, before leaving you, I have something to reveal to you." It concerned an exceptional grace he had received in Japan, when he had the joy of being assured of the salvation of his soul. Unfortunately, the religious who reported these testamentary remarks was not precise about the form of this mystical experience. According to several witnesses it might have been another apparition, to which they concede (I do not know why) more probability than to the first apparition, that of his childhood. It is a fairly good example of the "historical method". Regarding the first apparition, we have the testimony of Maria Kolbe; it is doubtful. The second is hypothetical; it is more believable.

"Thanks to what I tell you here," Kolbe continued, "in remembering my experience, your souls will ceaselessly progress in the religious life. Thus you will be able to withstand the sacrifices that God will demand of you, through the mediation of the Immaculata."

And there is the last peacetime letter, dated August 19, 1939, to the brothers at Nagasaki:

> I began to reply to the letters from Japan in June, but it is only now that I am finding a little free time to continue.
>
> As far as the war is concerned, here we are keeping our calm, but the state of alarm continues to augment daily. It is not out of the question that something will have happened by the time this letter reaches you, but all is in the hands of Divine Providence.

This something was the invasion of Poland—the beginning of the Second World War on September 1, 1939.

For some time, Kolbe had summed up the three stages of the religious life in three words: "Training, apostolate, and passion". His training had been perfect, his apostolate exceptionally productive. As for that passion, which it seems he had always known he would have to live one day, it was coming.

21

The Cause of Saints

Maximilian Kolbe was forty-five; he had two years left to live. The final phase of his life was to be as distinctly different from all that had preceded it as the last days of Christ were violently different from the prelude of teaching and relative peace. But before going into that final period we should ask a question: At the time he climbed his Calvary, was he already what the Church officially calls a saint?

In Rome, the congregation for the cause of saints sits in one of two great neo-something-or-other-style palaces that face each other at the end of the avenue leading to Saint Peter's, above the buses, taxis, and ice-cream vendors. Inside there are vast corridors wide enough to drive along, and in the offices, the usual furniture of religious houses, where credenzas alternate with file cabinets and plush with chrome.

It is there that saints are made. They lead a well-regulated life on the shelves of the archives and assembled in three volumes bound in red cloth: *The Inquest, The Objections,* and *The Responses.* It is the library of living faith and charity, the conservatory of the beauty of souls, the enclosure of virtue, and the garden of miracles.

One notices numerous and roomy voids on the shelves, as if the canonized saints, in an excess of Christian charity, had crowded together against the paneling to make room for new arrivals. Optimism? No, Napoleon. The voids are due to his passage. He ran off with the Vatican archives. For weeks, teams drew wagons past Saint Peter's, the memory of the Church leaving by the cartload. The only dossiers to escape the movers were those of the Holy Office, which the Pope had ordered burnt. They contained confessional secrets of crowned heads. The rest was seized, and the Church would be amnesiac had not France, after the Empire, generously let her buy back her own possessions, although that could be only partially done.

In these reconstituted archives one finds neither Saint Peter nor Saint Paul nor any of the saints of the early times. Then saint was synonymous with martyr, and witnesses to the Faith were venerated without any other form of trial. All the Christians buried in the catacombs were considered martyrs, which was not always the case. Besides, given the anonymity of most of the sepulchres, mistakes could be made. For example, today there is reason to believe that the famous and blessed Philomena worked the major part of her miracles through someone else's body.

For many years, the bishops had the right to proclaim anyone a saint who seemed to them to be one. They themselves were elevated on the altars they had built so that during the first centuries of Christianity there was such a proliferation of haloes that thought had to be given to regulating the distribution. Since the bishops had little by little gotten into the habit of having their decrees countersigned by the Pope, so that the saints of their choice would be honored by the whole Church, and not only in their diocese, Rome took advantage and fixed laws that would otherwise have been difficult to establish. The period of great persecutions was past and, in consequence, martyrdom was no longer the simple and radical criterion of sainthood. Thus it came about that we began to speak of the "heroism of virtue" as analogous to the heroism of the martyrs, a notion as exacting as it is relatively imprecise. To quote a Pope who took an interest in the dossier of a poor religious, relegated for forty years to the most obscure duties, the heroism of virtue may consist of "doing the most ordinary things in an extraordinary manner"—that is to say, acting with patience, abnegation, firmness in trials, and perseverance in good, as is seen in many religious and the majority of mothers of families, whose cases are never pleaded in Rome. As for Kolbe, one could say of him rather that he did extraordinary things in an ordinary manner.

In a thousand years, that is to say, since the rules of official sanctity were fixed, the Church has pronounced a thousand canonizations, about one each year, and 993 are in progress, about half of these being Italians. Italians are nearer to Saint Peter's; they know the house, and they go in the right door. Also, they know how to present a cause, better in any case than that American archbishop who was anxious to see the elevation of a holy man from his diocese, and who sent this telegram ahead when he went to Rome: "Prepare everything for the canonization. I'm on my way."

A canonization is a long-term process. Joan of Arc's lasted five hundred years, and Charles de Foucauld's has made no progress in years. On the line leading to sainthood, through trains are rare.

It is all begun by the *vox populi,* the reputation for sanctity arousing popular devotion. The bishop of the area then opens an inquest and assembles a dossier he will send to Rome if the cause seems worthy of support. From then on, the subject is called "the Servant of God". The inquest is taken up concerning his life, his foundations, and his writings and if Rome decides that because of heroic virtue there is reason to pursue the examination, "the Servant of God" becomes "Venerable". Writings may be held against him and never help his case in a decisive manner, the Church considering that one may write very well and behave as if one had never read one's own writings. Such is the case of the Benedictine Dom Marmion, who spoke marvelously of the vanities of the world but went to tea too often at the homes of duchesses; his halo stayed in his teacup, with the lemon.

The canonization procedure is less ferocious than the lions of the first centuries, but it is rigorous, prudent, and complex. The witnesses swear to tell the truth, and those who break their oath risk an excommunication that only the Pope can rescind. There are commissions that are as much tribunals; a postulator, who presents the cause with the help of a lawyer; a promoter general of the Faith, better known as the "Devil's Advocate", whose mission is to reveal the weaknesses in the dossier or, on the contrary, to reject the ill-founded observations of consultants who express themselves in writing and of experts who examine miracles. When all the evidence is studied, all the witnesses heard, the Pope decides, in total sovereignty. If his judgment is favorable, the "Venerable Servant of God" is proclaimed "Blessed". That is beatification. Next comes what is called "the testimony of God", as the miracles are called. At least one miracle is needed for beatification and another for canonization.

Certain candidates are fertile in marvels, others less so. Pius XII, who is generally considered to have lived in an exemplary manner, has worked no miracles. John XXIII has worked almost more than anyone has asked of him and even before the heroic nature of his virtues had been officially established. Martyrs are exempted from performing miracles, and the autopsy of their personality is not pushed as far as in the case of "confessors of the Faith". Their death may be considered as a baptism of blood, which becomes the day of their real birth. However, the circumstances of their death are examined with redoubled meticulousness.

Maximilian Kolbe, having been, as we have seen at the beginning of this volume, beatified as a "confessor of the Faith" by Pope Paul VI and then canonized as a "martyr" by Pope John Paul II, had therefore been subjected to two processes. The first was on the heroism of his virtue and the second on his sacrifice, so to speak, one on his life, the other on his death. The moment has come to conclude the first.

Today the Devil's Advocate walks the corridors of the palace of the saints with a melancholy expression. The new rules of the Congregation have taken away his job; he has become the theologian (par excellence, of course), and his former attributions have been divided between the eminent reporters. However, at the time of Maximilian Kolbe's process, he still exercised his function of supreme examiner to the full extent. All the pieces of evidence in the dossier having passed through his hands, it was in his power to draw up a report of perfection or insufficiency on the life and work of the defendant that would be submitted to the judgment of the Holy Father. He shows up fairly often in those pages, his finger pointed to what he considered a failing or an error, but truth to tell, his summation had not much grist to grind.

To begin with, he observed that witnesses projected the brilliant light of Kolbe's death on his life retrospectively, which resulted in an idealization of his person in which "collective and uncontrolled" enthusiasm lost both moderation and discernment.

"As all great historical events need a hero," he said, "the last worldwide conflict found its hero in Kolbe, standing against the background and in the frame of Poland, which, among all the nations, came out of the war the most cruelly tortured."

The Devil's Advocate would keep that moderation; he would not lose self-control. Kolbe, in his eyes, was incontestably driven by a great desire to perfection, but his progress seemed to be hindered by his individualism, a stubborn character, a sentimental and romantic disposition, the extravagant imagination of a knight errant (read: fanciful), his nationalism, and so on. All of this, if it made him one of the most interesting personalities, even as has been said, "one of the richest and most fascinating of our time", put him outside the classic outline of sanctity (renunciation of self, a continual effort to correct and rise above one's own nature so as to attain an equilibrium of virtue in harmony with a higher plan) while putting him in contradiction with the rule and the constitutions of his order.

The "closing remarks" of the Devil's Advocate are entirely on this theme. Kolbe was "a personality *sui generis,* somewhat disconcerting", in polite society one would call him an eccentric. But Saint Francis of Assisi was another, and when he stripped naked in a public square he too burst out of the "classic outline of sanctity".

We have already come across the remarks made by the prosecution about the way in which Kolbe lived the virtues of faith, hope, and charity and the accessory virtues of prudence and humility. That he practiced them to the point of heroism was evident to even the Devil's Advocate himself, who was an honest man and, after having criticized in the role of a reticent examiner, ended as a judge won over by the accused. He lowered his flag, but he said:

> At the moment I lowered my sails, I felt the need to declare that, finding myself on the opposite side, it was not without difficulty that I resisted the fascination exerted by the figure of this "sublime fool", with whom one breathed the very pure air of the heights. I was convinced that the diligent postulator of the cause would find valid arguments to dissipate the shadows and put Maximilian Kolbe, illustrious son of Saint Francis and the order of Conventual Friars Minor, in the best light.

The first process on Kolbe would have been peaceful, and the defense would not have had, so to speak, to raise its voice to win the case on the question of virtues. The second process, on his status as martyr, would be stormier, the opposition more categorical, the defense less at ease. After having passed beyond the "classic outlines of sanctity", Maximilian Kolbe was going to pass beyond those of martyrdom. But we are going to enter the first circle of his passion, which begins with that of his homeland.

22

Do Not Forget Love

On September 1, 1939, Hitler broke through the Polish border, hurling his tanks against the Polish cavalry, as heroic as ever and massacred as usual. The Allies declared war against Germany and did not wage it. The British navy barely raised the pressure in its boilers. The French army, considered at that time the strongest in the world, sank into the Maginot Line and could not move, cemented alive. English and French, immobile, watched the dismemberment of the still-warm victim by Hitler and Stalin, who had advanced to take Poland from behind and finish her off. In the face of this crime against people protected by only the paper of treaties, the universal conscience stammered its reprobation, while the shivering bourgeois democracies still hoped that the dragon, sated, would forget to turn its head their way.

On September 5, 1939, the machinery of Niepokalanow stopped; the hurricane was approaching. The German air force bombarded Warsaw and, in passing, dropped a few bombs on the Marian city, doing little damage and hurting no one. However, the civil authorities ordered Kolbe to disband the community. The six or seven hundred religious of the largest monastery in the world were about to disperse into thin air, after having received from their superior all the encouragements in which his faith was so rich, the accessory counsels to avoid alcohol and tobacco, and, on the doorstep, this final recommendation: "Do not forget love!"

About forty of the brothers had refused to leave and stayed close to Kolbe in the depopulated monastery, where there could now be heard only the murmur of prayers and bad news. With the Polish lines of defense giving way one after the other, they wondered what their fate would be. Would they be arrested, tortured, shot, or hit by the bombs, which had already claimed many victims in the neighborhood? Kolbe had enlarged his infirmary for them. By September 12 there was no more front; the green wave swept over the country. Each morning after Mass Kolbe prepared his companions for the worst. On the nineteenth of September the German trucks came to take delivery of the remaining resisters of the exodus, with the exception of two of them authorized by grace not to abandon the wounded. A photograph, taken by one of those numerous soldiers of the Wehrmacht who never missed an opportunity to enrich their photo albums with the bad memories of others, shows us a thin column of habits and black hats leaving Niepokalanow with, at its head, a sick man leaning on a cane. It is Kolbe, going toward the unknown as if he were going on mission and for once, he said, without having to pay for the trip.

The trucks stopped at Częstochowa, in the great avenue that leads to the shrine, which was considered a favor if not a promise of destiny. Six hundred civilian prisoners joined the brothers, and the soldiers pushed everyone into a train headed for Germany. They would arrive five days later, with a reputation for being fighters furnished by the Nazi propaganda, at the village of tents, barbed wire, and watchtowers of the concentration camp of Amtitz. The eliminatory deportation had not yet gotten to its industrial stage, but the regimen of the camp, if it was not deliberately exterminatory, was already tolerably degrading. The starved prisoners waded around in the mud, slept on straw, and struggled with vermin, bad morale, and the false charge of being troublemakers, which made the warden suspicious. Kolbe never stopped fortifying their faith, never suspecting that one day his own faith would be learnedly debated, and as he slept poorly, he went about arranging the covers on those who slept. Sometimes his solicitude roused them, and they were astonished by his humble attention. But for him, a minute of wakefulness was a minute not to be lost. His only fear was that he might let an opportunity for charity pass by. He would not have it again in heaven, where he said one can no longer suffer for love. Such is the unique apprehension of saints.

Kolbe announced to his companions their coming liberation through the good offices of the Immaculata, and they listened, their feet wet, their bellies empty, with a confidence mitigated by the first frosts of autumn. After having raised their morale, he went to talk to the soldiers and their commander about their souls. The commandant, it seems, was not insensitive to the language of faith. Then they were sent off to another place of internment, nearer to their fatherland. It was situated in the German area of Schildberg, since become Polish, as an effect of one of those lateral displacements to which Polish geography was subject. It was a monastery; the Salesians had been expelled or imprisoned elsewhere. The shelter was less precarious than the tents at Amtitz, but the regimen was no better and official calories as rare.

However, the commandant, a Protestant pastor in civilian life, was not an uncompromising jailer, and from time to time he permitted the prisoners to go into town to get food under the surveillance of two soldiers. Really, and his letters bear it out, he was deeply impressed by Father Kolbe. The latter tranquilly pursued his mission and reiterated his optimistic prophecies, which would in the end be fulfilled. One December morning the commandant assembled three hundred of his inmates, among them the Franciscans, to inform them that they were being sent home. Then he went toward Kolbe to give him, with great ceremony, as one might present a decoration before the troops, the best thing he had to give: two hundred grams of margarine. In exchange for this viaticum, the commandant immediately received a Miraculous Medal, which he would keep, but he made the mistake of not wearing it around his neck. It was blown up in his baggage toward the end of the war by an American shell, shells being lacking in discernment.

And this day when the followers of Mary saw their prison doors open was December 8, the Feast of the Immaculate Conception.

After several rail detours, Kolbe and his companions found their way back to Niepokalanow. At the entrance, the statue of Mary lay on the ground in scattered pieces. The church had been ransacked, the offices pillaged, with the exception of a few aged machines and broken pieces of furniture. The brothers, dismayed, looked at Kolbe, wondering what his reaction would be to seeing his work ravaged. But he was already planning its restoration. His most beautiful work, and that which could not be annihilated, was not his monastery but himself.

23

The Reprieve

Of course, no explanation had been given to the temporary deportees for their internment. At the same time, thousands of priests had been arrested throughout Poland by the occupying forces, who wanted to be free to occupy without having to be aware of certain individuals who had the influence to maintain among their compatriots a hope that was contrary to the rules of total war. If some of them had been liberated, it was either because the army, solidly entrenched in the area, had been persuaded that they had nothing more to fear from them or because, according to a wilier calculation, the security police thought that they would assemble around them resistance groups that would be easier to locate than others.

Kolbe's correspondence, interrupted by that painful excursion behind the barbed wire, which sprung up like crabgrass on the territories occupied by the Reich, took up again in December 1939 with a letter "to the officer of the German district of Sochaczew" in which Niepokalanow was located. He asked of this personage, who held simultaneously all powers, the authorization to resume publication of *The Knight,* which implied the removal of the seals placed on the old presses disdained by those who had looted the monastery. The reasons he put forth brought out the underlying motives for the sort of very obvious political neutrality that he would observe during the short time he had left to live.

> The aim of this magazine [he wrote (in pencil, as the definitive text would have to be translated into German)] is solely the diffusion among souls of love and devotion to the Immaculata. We believe firmly that she is living in paradise and that she loves every soul on this earth, but all souls do not know her love or recollect it as deserved. . . . We wish to speak to all souls living in the world, in all languages, to describe the graces she pours into hearts. . . . Until now, The *Knight* has been published only in Latin, Polish, Italian, and Japanese, while the inscription blanks for the Marian Militia are printed in thirteen languages, to wit: Polish, English, Arabic, Czech, Latin, Flemish, Dutch, Japanese, French, Latvian, German, Portuguese, and Italian. However, in time, we would like to omit no language commonly spoken on the earth.
>
> *The Knight* is at the exclusive service of love, and if by chance it happens to lack, even slightly, Christian charity, this would be contrary to the spirit of the "Militia" and to the intentions of the superiors of our order.
>
> Politics play no part in the goals of the "Militia", as the attached statutes show. Consequently *The Knight,* which is its official publication, does not have anything to do with politics either.

For Kolbe, the only thing to be saved, in this world where one saw more and more clearly the hideous jaws of Moloch coming out of the shadows of a new barbarism, was love, which fed on faith just as hatred fed on itself. That love that came from God, and over which no one here below had the least power, would establish among pure hearts a network of complicity like that which linked the Christians in the catacombs. That is why Kolbe did not turn Niepokalanow into a center of political resistance that could have been demolished a quarter of an hour after having been led, as no doubt would have happened, to sacrifice the Gospel to efficacy from time to time. In that Poland concentrated in its Faith like the Body of Christ can be in a fragment of Host, its line of resistance passed through loving souls and transcended the calamity and oppression of the invaders that Poles ironically called "our guests".

Three months later, Kolbe renewed his demand to the same officer, with new arguments:

> In one or two hundred years, you and I will no longer be alive. Then all our problems will be settled, even the most important, and only one will remain: Will we still exist at that moment, and where? Will we be happy? It is the same for all men. Every hour brings us closer to that moment. Our review deals with this kind of problem.

He goes on to explain that "the most Holy Virgin Mary is not a fable but a living being who loves each one of us". However, she and her love are not known well enough. He does not feel, he says, hatred for anyone on earth, and this sentiment is unknown in his monastery; if anyone wishes to assure himself on this point, he should come to visit.

The officer of the district filed the letter. The Virgin Mary was not under his jurisdiction, and he was not curious about where he would be in a hundred years.

On May 21, 1940, Kolbe wrote to the dispersed brothers: "Dear sons. A single act of perfect love makes a soul reborn. In practice it is not so difficult, for the principle of such an act is love ready for sacrifice; let us seek to please the

Immaculata by paying with ourselves, without thought of the recompense or the punishment." A résumé of activities at Niepokalanow followed.

While waiting for the authorization to print, which did not come, Kolbe had transformed his "publishing monastery" into a care center to assist the local population, housing refugees, doing mechanical repairs, and producing food. Each day, the infirmary received sixty or seventy persons, who were furnished with medicines from the monastery's little pharmacy or gathered in the hospital they had installed in a building. The mechanical workshop repaired machines and farm tools for the local peasants. The carpentry workshop repaired or made tables, chairs, benches, ladders, egg crates, and rowboats for the communications department. The brother tailors made new habits; the shoemakers resoled old shoes or made new ones. The brother cooks prepared, three times a day, meals for the fifteen hundred refugees, who ate the bread from the bakery and occupied almost the whole monastery. The brother gardeners planted cabbages, tomatoes, cucumbers, and potatoes in every piece of cultivable land. They fixed clocks and made cheese, and as it was not possible to forget why one had entered this monastery and since it was not possible to procure those precious articles elsewhere, they moulded plaster statuettes of the Immaculata, without knowing what would be done with them on this earth.

At the beginning of summer 1940, the Western democracies had lost the French army, destroyed or imprisoned, and England alone stood against Hitler, with the help of a few volunteers, survivors of the military disasters on the continent and determined never to surrender. The Nazi flag now floated over eight capitals, with its black insignia in the deathly form of a gear. In Poland, there was no law other than that of the conquerors, who were slowly putting in place their system for executing or enslaving the conquered. At Niepokalanow, Kolbe—it was barely easier to discourage him than to reduce him to inactivity—directed, often from his sickbed, the hundred religious and the new enterprise he had built on the debris of the old one. This little Franciscan, so long misjudged, might have taken the phoenix for his emblem. Demolish his work, and it would be reborn next day in another form. Limit the perimeter of his action, and he would act in depth. Close his press; he would open a canteen. Silence him, and his generous hands would say what his mouth could no longer say. Forbid him to express his faith; he would cultivate hope, and the charity that had come through his writings now came through his hospital.

During the year 1940, the Kolbe system of recovery of routed love functioned to the fullest. From December 1939 on he had been in a position to welcome thirty-five hundred refugees from the Poznan region. Among them were fifteen hundred Jewish refugees. After the war, you could not talk to the survivors about Kolbe's "anti-Semitism". Niepokalanow had been their last experience of goodness and fraternity on this earth. With regard to the Jews, the only error Kolbe made was to let himself be upset for a while by a falsehood, the "Protocol of the Sages of Sion", a supposed international pact to monopolize power concluded between imaginary Jewish conspirators. In his time, many people had been misled by this forgery. But it never prevented Kolbe from receiving the Jews with open arms or from running after them to remind them of the rights and duties of their election. Those who were at Niepokalanow, in any case, testified their gratitude in writing.

The occupying power used the Kolbe complex as a charitable institution coupled with a transit station, and they sent him Poles, Jewish or Catholic, and also *Volksdeutschen,* that is to say, "German-speaking expatriates recovered in the conquered countries being regrouped before being taken back to Germany or established in annexed regions". Kolbe took this advantage to obtain ration coupons and the permission to reassemble the dispersed religious. When their resources were exhausted, the brothers traversed the countryside and begged for those who had nothing from those who had little. In his letters, Kolbe called all the refugees by their proper name: they were deportees, with the possible exception of the *Volksdeutschen.* The only uncertainty, for the moment, was their destination.

The months passed, and finally the authorization arrived to publish one issue of *The Knight.* Printed on the presses disdained by the spoilers of the monastery, it came out for the Marian feast on December 8, with three texts by Kolbe. The first is a statement by the editor defining the intentions of the magazine and proposing, with resolute optimism, subscriptions free for those who could not pay. The second piece sang the glory of Mary on the occasion of the Feast of the Immaculate Conception, a date often marked, in Kolbe's life, by a happy event—or a sad one. The third text, entitled "The Truth", is a sort of coded message, easily read. It could be taken as an inoffensive exposé on the benefits of the principle of identity ("A is A"), that I cannot affirm one thing and deny it at the same time, and when there are innumerable contradictors to support the contrary the truth is not affected, because it is as powerful as it is unique. No one knows how to change it; one can only seek it, find it, recognize it, and conform one's life to it. The happiness that all men seek in this world can only be built on it; without truth such happiness is no more durable than the lie—and that goes for all of humanity just as for each person.

These edifying facts, apparently inoffensive, went straight against the basic principles of the Nazi system, which was built, like all totalitarian regimes, on a statutory indifference to what was true or false and on a permanent convertibility of good and evil.

The district officer doubtless soon regretted his authorization. That article was the last Kolbe would ever write.

24.

The Arrest

After several months' stay at Niepokalanow, certain of the guests whose status was undecided were authorized to find a stable location. Others were sent to reside in such and such a region of their country. The most unfortunate were sent to camps; there was reason to be fearful, but no one knew precisely why. The truth about the Nazi concentration camps was still not well known. The author of this book, imprisoned by the Gestapo in the "Jewish dump" at Fort Montluc in Lyons and as well informed about the Nazi methods as it was possible to be, still thought in 1943, as did his companions in captivity, that the camps were sort of open-air prisons, with more work and fewer shootings. The Jews who were deported thought that they were escaping the massacres of hostages that periodically depopulated the "dump", and they left with the illusions of the prisoner believing the penal colony preferable to the prison.

While Kolbe, with the help of the brothers, more and more numerous, labored relentlessly to strengthen his work, the occupying power did its best to distort it. Munitions were stored in one of the buildings, which furnished a good pretext for putting more guards on the others. The Gestapo, suspecting that the refugees lacked respect for the Reich, made frequent incursions into the monastery and put agents there, who were soon spotted, but they made up injurious reports, as was expected of them. Kolbe prayed for them and hung medals on them, just as he did with the soldiers on guard. Saint Francis of Assisi preached to the birds; Kolbe preached to the German eagles, with less success. The journalists came from the German daily in Warsaw. They were politely received, tasted the soup, left, and published an article denouncing Niepokalanow as a nest of political resistance. An administrative officer of the district showed up one day with his mistress and pushed this gaudily dressed woman into Kolbe's room, somewhat like the entourage of Saint Thomas Aquinas assigning him a professional companion to take his mind off metaphysics and bring him back to the usual diversions of people his age. Saint Thomas sent the creature fleeing with a red-hot poker. This time the temptress got off with a sermon and the procurer with a lesson on ecclesiastic celibacy.

Another visit might have had greater consequences, and it did. During the summer, emissaries of the district, appointed by the authorities in Warsaw, using as an argument the Germanic consonance of his name and his knowledge of the language, offered Kolbe German citizenship. If he accepted, he would become a *Volksdeutscher,* one of these nationals from outside whom he had sheltered in his monastery. He would be safe from arbitrary arrest, he would obtain all the administrative facilities to continue his work, and his relative immunity might extend to the entire monastery. But you will remember that Kolbe, as a child, wept when his little friends teased him about his surname because it seemed too German to be Polish. The emissaries, who did not understand how anyone could hesitate to pass from the status of occupied to that of occupier, had the surprise of hearing their offer refused.

For the Devil's Advocate, this good patriotic reflex was not to be taken into account in the beatification process.

On several occasions, since the return from Amtitz, Kolbe's companions had begged him to seize one of the opportunities to escape that were provided by the unforeseen incidents of travel. They could see that he was more in danger than any of them because of his physical fragility and because of his responsibilities, which made him more conspicuous. They believed him to be indispensable to the order, to the Church, to their own hope, and his insistence in repeating that he would not see the end of the war terrified them. But what they called escape, he called abandoning his post. He would not dream of it.

During Kolbe's last three months of liberty, the oppression did not cause his spiritual course to deviate one jot, and the tone of his letters did not change. Imperturbable, he spoke with even humor about everything: "It seems to me that we cannot merely make a loan to nor demand security of those who ask our help: if possible, we must give them what they need.

"Let Divine Providence do as it will. . . . Many, who once swam in abundance and hardly thought of eternity, are more concerned about their souls now that they have become poor."

"Life in this world is not long. The most important thing is to prepare well for eternity. This speck of dust in the universe that we call the earth will end, and all the problems will end with it."

"Do not worry about your hair. Our father Saint Francis of

Assisi did not go about with a comb and mirror in his pocket. One cannot imagine him with a cigarette in his mouth either."

"The consecration to Mary is for the intrepid hearts and those who do not fear adversity or betrayal, for there is not a representation of the Virgin Mary where one does not see the serpent beneath her feet."

"Faced with suffering and humiliation, human nature is frightened, but in the light of faith, they should be welcomed with gratitude for the purification of our soul!"

"In the middle of storms, both external and internal, we need to stay very, very calm. This is what the apostles lacked when they were at sea and the storm raged against their boat. In fact, once the storm was over, Jesus reproached them for having such little faith (Mt 8:26)."

"The problem of peeling potatoes has been resolved." (The Germans made each religious peel sixty potatoes per day. . . . Kolbe had probably invented a machine.)

"Very dear Mama! I am trying to obtain the authorization to print a new edition of *The Knight* in February [1941]."

"I had dreamed of having my bones put in the foundation of the Japanese Niepokalanow. But who knows where humanity will want me to leave them one day?"

"Very Reverend Father, . . . as to the formation [of the young religious] . . . the system of the cane hardly suits me. In all nature, the development of life is encouraged rather by sun and dew."

"At this time, we are mostly engaged in manual work, to help the residents of the area, especially the poor."

Finally, to Cornelius Kaczmarek, address Dachau: "You are alive, thanks to God and the Immaculata." Following is a description of the different activities at Niepokalanow, where a Red Cross medical unit had been installed for some time to care for the Polish prisoners of war.

It was Kolbe's last letter as a free man, or rather a man on probation.

Kolbe's refusal to accept German citizenship, the reports of the spies, justifying the police confidence by lies, could not remain without effect. The Gestapo, who mistrusted any charitable organization whose director declined the honors of integration into the great Reich, summoned a brother who had been expelled recently from Niepokalanow. He had had the unfortunate idea of making counterfeit money. They interrogated him about the imaginary subversive activities of Father Kolbe and made him sign a statement saying in German—a language he did not speak—the opposite of his declaration in Polish. At least that is what this witness always stated later. Whatever happened, his deposition, falsified or not, became a redoubtable piece of evidence against Kolbe.

Elsewhere, in February 1941, Hitler was preparing his great offensive against Russia, which was to have taken place in May and was delayed by Mussolini's blunder. Mussolini's greed for conquest catapulted him into the Greek trap, where his army would have perished without the help of the German troops. But although delayed, the assault against Stalin was no less close, and Hitler methodically trampled Poland and her people underfoot so as to maneuver at his ease, while on the other side of the partition line Stalin filled the ditches of Katyn with Polish officers. The two greatest liars in contemporary history were face to face. Strangely, the oriental liar, who distrusted everyone, gave credence to a rag of a treaty signed with the occidental liar, who lied so as to inspire confidence. Stalin did not believe the reports announcing the imminent arrival of the tanks.

For Hitler, it was a matter of protecting the rear of his future Russian countryside and of rendering Poland totally impotent, not only by the brutal repression (stifling) of her last convulsive struggles and by the removal of bothersome or suspect populations but also by the preventive elimination of all those who could, one day or another, arouse or attract possible resistance movements: in general the elite, in particular the intellectuals and the priests—among them Kolbe. Between 1939 and 1945, these politics complemented by those of Stalin would kill six million Poles, Jews, and Catholics.

The evening of February 16, 1941, the eve of his arrest, Kolbe spoke with a small group of young disciples about the joy of being called to spill one's blood for one's ideal. Then he had a long conversation with five brothers from the early days at Niepokalanow, and they shared a cake, like the bread shared among the apostles in the cenacle. Then he retired to his cell but did not sleep. Almost as surely as Christ on the eve of his Passion, Kolbe knew that his hour had come.

At two o'clock in the morning, Kolbe woke a brother and prayed with him in his cell.

At four o'clock in the morning another brother received a visit and noticed the pallor of Kolbe's face.

That night, says the Gospel, on the Mount of Olives, in a place called Gethsemane, Jesus, who had prayed at a distance from his disciples, came back to them, found them asleep, and said to them: "My soul is sad unto death." Then he went away to pray, came back once more, and, finding them again asleep, he said to them: "Could you not watch one hour with me?"

At daybreak, Kolbe was warned of the approach of the police from Warsaw. He had friends even among the enemy.

Kolbe put on his Sunday habit, took care of some current business with a secretary, and waited.

At midmorning, the brother porter notified Kolbe by telephone that a cortège of black cars had just entered Niepokalanow. He put the receiver down and murmured: "Fine, Mary."

The police found Kolbe on his doorstep. He said: "Praised be Jesus Christ", according to the etiquette of monasteries. After having been assured of his identity, the police were surprised to hear him suggest a visit to the workshops. They accepted. The visit finished, they informed him of his arrest, claimed five other brothers, and only got four. The fifth, thought to be in Warsaw, was in his room, where no one thought to look for him.

When the prisoners got into the cars, a brother approached Kolbe and gave him a little buttered bread in a paper bag. Another, much younger, asked permission to accompany him. The police told him it was unnecessary, that Kolbe would be brought back.

Then, says the Gospel, he was handed over to the soldiers to be scourged.

25

Pawiak

We do not know if Father Kolbe was better informed about the reasons for his arrest the second time than he had been the first. There is no record of the interrogation, and it seems that when the Gestapo entered Niepokalanow they asked him only questions about his teaching. In effect, the training of priests had recently been forbidden in Poland.

Kolbe was taken, with his four companions, to the Pawiak prison, as famous and as feared in Warsaw as the Lubianka was in Moscow. They were thrown into a common cell with thirty or so prisoners, all maimed or lacerated. They were waiting to be judged—a dubious advantage—deported, or finished off by the police. Then they were separated and locked up in different parts of the prison.

Whether in the common cell or a smaller one, Kolbe was Kolbe. More concerned with others than with himself, he accepted his imprisonment as a mark of providential affection, to be lived without complaint. All he cared about was making a little hope sprout in this sterile setting.

The penitentiary administration authorized the prisoners to

send news of themselves, on condition that it was good and written in German. Niepokalanow received six letters from Kolbe; one of them was a simple printed form where the sender could only sign his name.

> February 24. Will you please send to each of us, in a cardboard box: one shirt, one pair of shorts, two pairs of socks, two small towels, two handkerchiefs, a toothbrush, and toothpaste. These five packages, addressed to each of us separately, should be taken to the seventh commissariat, on Krochmalna Street. Near the addressee's name, write the names of his relatives (or the senders). I would ask you also to send each of us a postal order for ten zlotys (for stamps).

> March 13. My dear son [his replacement at Niepokalanow]: I received the postcard of March 4 and a second package of linen. Do not send any office supplies, or other packages, except at my express request. Take care of your health. All the brothers pray much and well, work, and are not sad, because nothing can happen without the knowledge and assent of the good Lord and the Immaculate Virgin.

> April 2. My dear son: Thanks for your card of March 22. I had previously received a card from Brother Arnold, to which I had already replied. The money also arrived. I thank the Virgin Mary that all goes well for you there and that you are all trying to carry out your duties. For some time I have been in the infirmary because of a fever. Brother Batosik [he would die at Auschwitz] had pneumonia with a high fever, but now he is well, although somewhat weakened. As for the food packages for Easter, inquire at the seventh commissariat of the Polish police. They should be addressed to each of us separately, because we are not together. It would be good if we each received two or three postcards, so that we can reply. My most cordial greetings to all, with the earnest request for your prayers.

> May 1. [This was the printed form.] I am permitted to receive food packages of five kilos twice a month. They should be taken to the seventh commissariat of police, at 56 Krochmalna Street, the fifth and the twentieth of each month, between noon and six o'clock. Present this paper at the office.

> May 1. My dear ones: I received the Easter package, as well as the cards from Brothers Freilich, Ivo, and Arnold. Thanks. I rejoice that you have much work. Thanks be to God and the Immaculate Virgin, that loving Mother who will care for her children, in the future as in the past. I have already left the infirmary, but I am still receiving hospital rations. Currently I am assigned to the library. Today begins the beautiful month of May, dedicated to the Mother of God. I hope that you will not forget me in your prayers.

The last letter:

> May 12. My dear ones: Send me civilian clothing. I am writing this at the commandant's order. Coat and pants are not necessary; those that I have are still in good condition. Send me work clothes (warm) with a sweater that buttons up, a shawl, or a scarf. Very urgent! I received your package of the fifth and the letters from Brothers Felix and Pelage. The Immaculata will reward you. I cannot reply to each of you individually, because I am not permitted to write more often, but in my cards I mention each letter, card, or package received from you. Let us always be led, ever more obediently, by the Immaculata where she wishes, so as to fulfill our duties, all souls being won over to her love. Cordial greetings and best wishes to all and to each.

He signed "Raymond Kolbe", in conformity with his civil status. For the German police he was not Father Maximilian.

Meanwhile, twenty brothers from Niepokalanow had written to the Gestapo to propose that they be allowed to take Kolbe's place in prison. They declared themselves ready to take on themselves all the charges pressed against him and to suffer the consequences. The innocence of pure hearts. The Gestapo could not but reject the offer and tighten its claws on the catch that everyone so wanted to snatch from them.

Kolbe had been beaten. A Schauführer, a sergeant, belonging doubtless to that hybrid species of Sicherheitsdienst, or "security service", a cross between the Gestapo and the SS, pounced on Kolbe one day, snatched the rosary he wore on his belt, and, showing him the crucifix, demanded to know if he really believed in it. Kolbe having responded, "Yes", the Schauführer struck him in the face. Then he repeated his question several times, and as he obtained the same response each time, he struck each time. When he left, Kolbe's comrades, seeing him praying, approached to comfort him. But he told them not to worry about him, that what had happened was nothing, that he withstood those things without pain for love of Mary. He continued his prayer, and, according to the witnesses, had not his face been red from the blows, one would have thought that nothing had happened.

It was after this incident that Kolbe was ordered to get civilian clothes. Incidents of the same sort had already occurred in that prison, where the sight of a religious habit caused the Nazis' delirious hatred of priests to go to their heads.

Kolbe's order had tried several times to have him and the other brothers from Niepokalanow freed. But the religious orders, in permanent danger of sudden liquidation, were not very successful at interceding to the Gestapo, who insisted on countering all requests with the "testimony" extracted from the ex-brother counterfeiter (according to him, falsified).

At the beginning of the month of April, Kolbe's four

companions, who had been in separate cells at Pawiak, had been deported to Auschwitz. He probably knew, for all prisons have ears. May 28 would be his turn.

Then, says the Gospel, the soldiers put the cross on his back and led him to a place called, in Aramaic, Golgotha.

26

Auschwitz

I come now to the unthinkable and the unforgivable, to the suffering of the innocent, to the far-off sobs of mothers carried away by a storm of grief, to those hills of shoes removed from children who were a smile, and then soot. I come to the hopeless moaning of despair and to insults to creation, to those funereal hectares of Cain with their silent passersby from beyond, who wander in our memory, their mouths full of earth. I come to speak of Auschwitz, the damp plain with indefinite boundaries, where the earth evaporates, where the fog draws its shrouds over the memory of those poor beings who tried in vain to protect with fleshless hands their last spark of life, breathing more and more feebly the poisoned air filled with lethal fumes and the last gasps of the dead.

There finished humanity.

A grilled gate surmounted by a banner carrying a sort of snigger in wrought iron: "Work makes free", opened on the colorless zone of an immense annihilation factory with its watchtowers, its gardens of concrete pillars and its vegetation of barbed wire stretching beyond view in the fog or the clouds of acrid smoke from the cremations.

Anyone who passed through this gate entered into his agony.

After several months, he was barely more than a skull sitting atop a pile of vertebrae stretching rumpled parchment. His eyes were no more than dull, vacant cavities where a last ember of distrust or terror smoldered. The administrative reports called him a "head". He was a former human being, led from reduction to reduction to the linear state of a sketch of a skeleton. Some did not last three weeks. The women died right away on getting down from their freight cars, terrified by the dogs and the uniforms, suffocated by the despair of being separated from their children, of no longer having anyone to live for, to be handed over, alone and stripped, to the examination of eyes that did not belong to our species and stared with the fixity of glass eyes.

And it was all a lie, from the inscription at the entry marked with that stamp of derision that decorates all works of evil to the musicians' platform facing the gallows.

The long buildings in the streets that led nowhere were not houses but canneries of manpower where sleep was only the exhausted wait for day, which awoke the nightmare. The honest little barracks with their tile roofs did not shelter soldiers but the expeditionaries of nothingness set up by Heinrich Himmler, who congratulated himself one day on their common habituation to massacre "that made them different from other men"—before losing consciousness himself during an extermination of prisoners organized expressly for him, like a dress parade organized for any important visitor. The experience prompted him to seek means of arriving at the same end that would be less trying for the executioners. These men, proud of an insensibility acquired from the daily exercise of murder, became, in effect, so "different" that the sentiments that mark the nobility and fragility of other men were foreign to them, and they believed that they dominated the human condition in the measure that they sank beneath it.

Another lie, the hospital that was not a hospital but a laboratory for preposterous medical and surgical research, a way-station for the dead in reprieve, lined up two by two, head to foot on narrow beds, waiting for nature or "selection" (meaning the syringe of a doctor) to put an end to their pain. It was a sanitary fiction intended to maintain among the prisoners the illusion that their lives were not just being systematically taken, that there did exist a refuge in the prison, and that they did have a chance, if not to escape, at least to find a gentle way out.

Lies, lies, the totalitarian systems that cannot stand to be contradicted either by morality, or by common sense, or by grace, or by nature feed on lies and holocausts.

The victims? The Jews, living mystery, chosen people, Christified by the Incarnation and going from Calvary to Calvary, pursued by those who do not pardon them for having given Christ to the world. The Christians, who did not want to give to Caesar what belonged to God, the unbelievers who refused to obey, to lie, to dishonor themselves in the service of the vile gods of race and blood. The gypsy, unfit for slavery and killed for that reason. The strong, who did not cheat their conscience; the weak, from whom there was nothing to take but miserable remnants of dignity and the yellow metal of a wedding ring or a tooth; and the children, crowds of Jewish children, who had not played long on the earth before being buried in it.

The debate about the ways and methods of extermination

is weird, odious, and vain. Who are those consciences who are unconscious of the realities, who do not see the evidence, who do not hear the moaning that still is heard today in the wind that stirs the poplars of Auschwitz? Everything, absolutely everything, and not only the rifles and the zyklon B, killed the prisoners. Malnutrition turned them over a period of time into sacks of skin filled with knucklebones. Standing unprotected at attention for several hours in the sun or in the swirling snow as it rushed in under the cloth caps and gripped the body with mortal cold. The work that was not work but the exploitation of the physical resources of the condemned, down to the last muscle spasm, for the benefit of the industries set up in the area. The bad treatment that left them here and there, crushed by blows from the overseer's club. These overseers were chosen from the underworld of the camp for their perfect amorality or the advantageously hysterical character of their servility. Illness, which only became worse, epidemics that ravaged the barracks without meeting any opposition.

And above all, the slow and detailed degradation of the person, dispossessed of his name in exchange for a number tattooed on his forearm, so that he could not deny his bondage if he succeeded in finding a way out of the forest of electric brambles. The person deprived of a future, his roots torn away, his memory no more than a focus of suffering, plagued by contempt, violence, and fear, attached to his own body as if to so much wreckage carried each day a little closer to the abyss; it was the person, the promise of eternity in man, that had to be destroyed.

And the crime did not begin, as some seem to believe, at the door of the gas chamber or on the edge of the common grave; it did not begin with the first cruelties of the camp or the shots administered by the pseudodoctors affiliated with the death's-heads of the SS, but much earlier. In truth, it was consummated, before God and before morality, from the moment a family was arrested and their destination was known. Individuals who go to lay hands on children are already murderers as they mount the stairs.

27

The Martyrdom

It was there, in that cloister of all agonies, that Kolbe was to die.

And then the question was asked: "Did he die a martyr?"

Thirty-five years after the war, the question would be asked of the tribunal of saints. Could the red crown of martyrdom be given to the little Franciscan who had wanted to save every man on earth?

Many felt so, in Poland, in Germany, in Japan, and elsewhere. In the manner of Saint Louis restoring Guyenne to the English "to make peace between the children of France and of England", German Archbishop Jaeger wrote an admirable letter to Pope John XXIII asking him to assist the cause "for our intimate and personal veneration of the servant of God, who died a martyr to Christian charity and the Catholic Faith, and to abolish all rancor between the noble Polish people and my nation".

But if the supporters of the proclamation of martyrdom were numerous throughout the world, in Rome they were more rare.

The Devil's Advocate, ready to concede the white crown,

stiffened suddenly when they spoke to him of the red crown.

The death of Kolbe left him perplexed. It seemed to him to be of the kind that makes a hero, not a martyr. He would allow, at the very most, that a monument should be erected for Kolbe, and one felt that if it was done he would be ready to contribute.

The theologians consulted were no more willing to give an inch. They went round and round about the traditional definition of martyrdom: "A witnessing to the Faith, unto death, inflicted out of hatred for the Faith", and they did not see how that could be applied to Kolbe. The defense had pointed out that today's persecutors do not have the good old-fashioned frankness to say to the Christian, "Renounce your God or die." They arrange for him to die for other reasons, liars about that as about all the rest. But there was nothing to be done. The theologians would not give in. The defense came to the point where they wondered if it would not be expedient to hold onto the white crown, which could be had without great difficulty.

However, John Paul II, supreme judge, was anxious that it be the red crown.

For him, the totalitarian systems are by nature and vocation "martyrogens". They place Christians, and all free men, in the same situation as the early Christians, enjoined to worship a deified Caesar. The Christian, or any free man, who does not consent and thus loses his life is a martyr. A believer dies for the Divine Person of Christ; a nonbeliever dies for the human person—which for him is similar.

And when it was pointed out to Pope John Paul II that in that case all the victims of the Nazi camps would have been martyrs and could be venerated as such, he did not deny it.

The Pope had received the opinions of the theologians

with interest, but he was no less attentive to the voice of the people, who sometimes recognize signs from God faster than do the specialists. He gave a verdict of martyrdom, to the great astonishment of Rome and of the tribunal that judges the dead. In his eyes, the sacrifice of Kolbe placed him well above debates. Is a process held to judge a candle, consumed to its very end by its flame?

Before announcing his decision, the Pope went to Auschwitz, where he stood frozen at the door of the dungeon where ten men had been condemned to starve to death. One of them had been a volunteer: Kolbe. Who could doubt that he was a saint and that he was a martyr, this man who had never lived except for others and who had, one day, like Christ, freely entered into his passion?

28

The Death of the Servant of God

The last letter written by Kolbe is dated Auschwitz, June 15, 1941. At that point, certain administrative rules were still respected at the camp. A register of the prisoners was kept, they were allowed to write, and sometimes notification of their death was sent to the family—official and untrue regarding the circumstances or the diagnosis. Then death, which overtook the trains, the cell blocks, and the hospital beds, carried away the rest, the registers, the civilian employees, the bookkeepers, and the undertakers. And who could have received letters from entire families taken, even to the babes in arms, and more often than not directed upon arrival to the "disinfecting" chambers, that lie on the signs labeling the extermination facilities?

Kolbe's letter was written in German on twenty short lines of ruled paper, preceded by forty lines of instructions about what was permitted (to receive money and newspapers on condition that they were "ordered through the Auschwitz post office") and forbidden (packages, "the prisoners can buy anything in the camp"—another lie—visits, petitions, and interventions on their behalf):

My beloved mother,

Toward the end of the month of May I arrived with a convoy at the Auschwitz concentration camp.

All goes well for me. Don't worry, dear Mama, about me and my health, for the good Lord is everywhere and thinks with much love about each of us.

It is better not to write to me here, because I do not know how long I will be staying.

Cordial greetings and kisses.

Raymond Kolbe

Kolbe had always shown himself to be, how can I put it, respectfully attached to his mother. In the thousand letters I looked over, though, I do not recall ever having seen mention of a kiss. She would die two years after the war with the memory of that tenderness and the peaceful certitude that she had given to the world, and to the Church, a witness to charity.

Head shaved and dressed in striped rags, Kolbe became number 16670, but everyone knew that he was a priest. The overseers who beat him and set their dogs on him knew too. There was among those individuals, and among the SS, a linked aversion for priests and Jews that made them persecute the two together as if they were the representatives of an identical, detestable religious conscience. And thus it happened that when a priest died, the guards had him thrown on a wheelbarrow and taken to the crematorium by a little cortège of Jews and "pigs of priests" forced to sing, behind a priest wearing a stole of dung and carrying a broom in place of a crucifix, while the guards on duty improvised enraged antiphons on the theme "there are no other gods but us!"

Kolbe was detailed to all sorts of work, exhausting and sometimes sinister. He was a porter hauling corpses with a fellow prisoner who, in another world, had been a minister of education. This man cringed as he handled the cadavers and nearly fainted at the gate of the crematorium. As he supported the minister, number 16670 prayed and blessed the smoke from the furnace.

This sick man dug the damp sand of the Sole, the river that ran past the camp, and his full shovel must have been heavier than he was. He pushed wheelbarrows full of gravel and lugged old stumps whose weight made him stagger, a weakness that was promptly punished. One day he was beaten senseless and left for dead by the guards. He was taken to the hospital, running a fever, his face swollen. He said nothing. He was given the last free place, in the draft at the door. He appreciated this. It allowed him to welcome the sick with a kind word and to pray for the dead as they were carried out.

In this camp, populated with shadows in the fog, in those twenty-eight blocks of barracks, those twenty-eight doomed rafts of *Medusa* becalmed in the shadows, everyone worked carefully at the delicate business of survival. It was crucial to avoid all useless effort, wind, and beatings and to make the slice of black bread that was the basis of the daily ration last twenty-four hours. A public prosecutor, who had perhaps condemned men for stealing chickens, was caught one night crawling about stealing bread.

In barracks 18, Kolbe occupied the bottom bunk of a bed. Without disturbing anyone, he could get up at night to go to hold the hands of the dying or to receive visits from those who could no longer stand their nightly encounter with death and needed to hear that the earth still existed.

Twelve survivors, twelve miracles, testified at the process. All of them described the same man, with brilliant eyes, so thin his bones nearly stuck through his prisoner's uniform, who carried his head on one shoulder, constantly ready to listen and invariably smiling.

All, Jews or Christians, priests or ministers, with death all around, saw Kolbe unconcerned about his own fate, too concerned with others to be worried about himself, and seeing everywhere those more unhappy and more pitiful than himself.

"Don't worry," Kolbe said to those who bandaged his wounds, "I can suffer a lot more than this."

Sometimes Kolbe shared his bread, and it was his life, his body that he gave.

It was hard to know from where that sickly, abused creature drew his force, or where that sick man found the hope that he distributed all around him as if it were Communion.

All twelve survivors were unanimous about Kolbe's way of suffering in silence and his apparent surprise when anyone showed him compassion after the brutalities that were so frequently inflicted on him.

For them Kolbe had been the dove after the flood, and the inquest about his heroism must have seemed a rather strange formality to them.

Kolbe had fallen into that evil enclosure where reality dissolved into nightmare like an unassailable fragment of the absolute.

He lived on what was refused him, he fortified himself with what should have crushed him, and when someone tried to humiliate him, he offered his honor for humanity.

What could they do to Kolbe? He lived his imprisonment like a special mission, his only concern that he might be unworthy of it.

The captives were prisoners of the reigning terror and of the insurmountable obstacles that separated them from the world. The overseers were prisoners of their base instincts, chained to their dogs, and the exuberance of their sadism did not succeed in hiding their terror that they might not be equal to the scorn of their masters. The SS were prisoners of their training for inhumanity, which rendered them deaf to all moaning, blind to all suffering, prisoners of their own commander, their boots, and their lies.

Number 16670, who had attained that ultimate state where abnegation bordered on the inalienable and the eternal, was the only one to move unfettered in that prison.

He alone was free.

"A prince among us", said one witness.

From time to time, there were escapes. Some succeeded; some did not. One fugitive was found hidden, naked, in a pile of cadavers. At Auschwitz that was one way to go unnoticed.

Toward the end of the war the escapes were fairly numerous. The "final solution to the Jewish problem" held the attention of the entrepreneurs of death, while the increase of work outside the camp furnished the survivors with opportunities to get hold of civilian clothes and find accomplices among the Polish population. But in 1941 the escapee was a rare specimen. One wonders if sometimes it was not a case of someone simply disappearing, drowning in the river, or being dead and forgotten in some ditch.

The reprisals, always disproportionate, varied over the years.

At this time for the life of one escapee the penitentiary monster took ten.

Ten men were condemned to die of hunger and thirst "until the fugitive was found". But that was another lie.

Whether or not the absent prisoner reappeared, the condemned remained condemned.

Toward the end of July, Kolbe was transferred to barrack 14, where they mostly put people out of the hospital. The rations were reduced in barrack 14. The least sickly were used for light gardening work or sent to harvest outside the camp.

Outside the net of barbed wire, out of sight of the watchtowers, escape became an affair of decision and opportunity.

The savage caterwauling of the sirens signaled one escape on the last day of the month, around three o'clock in the afternoon. The sirens not only alerted the guards but also carried far into the countryside and alerted the patrol.

After work, the whole camp remained standing in the exercise yard. It was ascertained that the missing prisoner belonged to barrack 14 and that he was a baker from Warsaw named Klos.

At nine o'clock they distributed a little soup, except to the prisoners in barrack 14, whose rations were thrown into the gutter. The order was then given to return to the barracks.

All night the prisoners maintained fragile hopes.

The next morning at dawn, after the coffee, all the prisoners left for work—the missing man was still missing. The six hundred prisoners from barrack 14 were kept standing immobile all day in the yard, in the blazing sun in rows of sixty, the smallest in the first row, the others behind. From time to time, one of them collapsed. At first they left the prisoners where they fell; then a crew came and piled them up to one side. It was forbidden to sit down, to talk, and, under pain of death, to get out of line. At three o'clock in the afternoon, there was a half-hour break, a little soup, and then back to standing in rows. At the evening roll call, along with guards and the dogs, came the assistant commandant of the camp, SS Karl Fritsch. He was accompanied by the adjutant SS Palitsch, who would one day boast of killing twenty thousand people, most of them with a rifle that had been modified to be less noisy and more efficient.

Commandant Fritsch announced to the prisoners that as the fugitive had not been found, ten of them were to be condemned to die of starvation in the bunker of barrack 11. Then he passed among the rows to choose his victims. He sometimes said: "Open your mouth. Show your teeth." And: "Out of line!" The adjutant Palitsch noted the numbers. Thus the little group of the condemned was formed.

It was then that something no one had ever seen happened: a prisoner dared to step out of line, to ask to take the place of another who wept and pleaded.

The prisoner was Kolbe. The little Franciscan had perhaps not succeeded in "converting the whole world", but his gesture would make all men his friends.

Of the twelve witnesses who knew Kolbe at Auschwitz and were heard during the process, one was not in the camp at that time, three others were busy elsewhere, one more, although present, saw and heard nothing, three others did not hear the words exchanged between Kolbe and Commandant Fritsch, and finally, one witness, the prisoner saved by Kolbe, spoke no German and could not follow the dialogue.

That left three witnesses who saw, heard, and understood. Each of them reported the facts in the same way with only slight differences (but there are such differences even in the Gospels). Two made mistakes about Kolbe's barrack number; either their memory failed them or the barrack numbers had been changed—barrack 11, for example, had been, for some time, barrack 14. Concerning the event itself, however, their accounts do not differ.

Here are their depositions, as recorded in the tribunal of saints.

The painter Miescislaw Koscielniak:

> The Servant of God died voluntarily in place of a companion in captivity, Francis Gajowniczek, father of a family. It was at the beginning of the month of August 1941. Because of the escape of a prisoner, the Lagerführer Fritsch ordered, as reprisal, the death of ten men.
>
> Our barrack was surrounded by guards with automatic rifles and dogs. The Lagerführer Fritsch himself chose the victims. I was in the third row, and I could see very well what happened. At one point, Fritsch pointed out the prisoner Francis Gajowniczek, who, terrified by death, begged to be spared.
>
> Then out of the ranks came a prisoner whom I recognized as Father Kolbe. The Servant of God approached Fritsch and in a calm voice declared in German that he wished to die in place of Francis Gajowniczek. Fritsch, irritated by the gesture of the Servant of God, put his hand on his revolver and demanded: "Have you gone mad?" Father Kolbe clearly repeated his request saying that his life was less useful than that of the other man, meaning Gajowniczek, who was the father of a family. After a short silence, Fritsch asked the Servant of God: "What is your profession?" Father Maximilian replied: "I am a Catholic priest." After another silence, Fritsch gave his consent and sent the Servant of God, with the group of prisoners destined to die, while Francis Gajowniczek returned to his rank.

Joseph Sobolewski, lawyer:

> The Servant of God offered himself up in the following circumstances: in camp, a prisoner had escaped from barrack 2.

The authorities ordered a search and threatened, in case thefugitive was not found, to condemn ten of his companions to die of starvation. The escapee not having been found, one evening at roll call, Commandant Fritsch, the Rapportführer Palitsch, and other SS chose ten prisoners to be sent to die of starvation in the bunker. Just behind me there were two prisoners from barrack 2 among those who would be chosen for the ten condemned. I saw perfectly what happened. At one point a prisoner was chosen, and as he stepped out of line he began to lament his fate desperately, crying that he had a wife and children and yet he was to die. This prisoner joined the little group of the other designated prisoners, to the right. After him there were two or three others chosen, and then it was finished. The commandant of the camp and the other SS were about to move away from the men of barrack 2 when, from the group, the Servant of God suddenly came forth and said to the overseer that he must speak to the commandant. The overseer ordered the Servant of God to get back into line, but he did not obey and insisted on speaking to the commandant. The SS who were near the commandant informed him. He then turned toward the Servant of God and asked him: "What do you want?" The Servant of God replied that he wanted to die in place of the prisoner who was in such despair at leaving his wife and children. The commandant asked him his profession. He replied that he was a priest. Then the commandant ordered him to go with the group of condemned men. The Servant of God went quickly toward the group and the desperate man returned to the ranks.

Doctor Niceto Wlodarski:

> It happened that at the end of July or the beginning of August, a prisoner escaped from the garden detail, I be-

> lieve. This escapee not having been found, the camp authorities decided to choose ten prisoners from barrack 2. During roll call, I was separated from the Servant of God by three or four persons. The Lagerführer Fritsch, accompanied by Rapportführer Palitsch and other SS, chose ten prisoners, among them Francis Gajowniczek. When this man learned what was to happen to him, he began to cry with pain and despair that he had a wife and children, that he wanted to see them again, and that he was going to die.
>
> At that point, Father Maximilian Kolbe stepped out of line, lifted his cap, and declared to the Lagerführer, pointing to Gajowniczek, that he wanted to sacrifice himself for that prisoner, as he had no wife and children. The Lagerführer asked him his profession. He replied: "I am a Catholic priest." There followed a moment while the SS showed a certain surprise. Then Fritsch ordered Gajowniczek to get back in line and the Servant of God to take his place among those condemned to the bunker.

For his part, the Polish sergeant Gajowniczek had seen Father Kolbe step out of line, an outrageous initiative. However, as he did not speak German, he did not understand what had happened until he was told to go back to his place. He is still alive.

From the window of a nearby building, a prisoner had watched the whole scene. He saw the SS push the little group of condemned men toward barrack 11. Maximilian Kolbe walked last, supporting a comrade. All were barefooted. They had been ordered to leave their galoshes in the yard.

Barrack 11, whose courtyard was surrounded by a very high wall, was where the interrogations and "executions", or murders, took place. One mounted a sill several steps high, then went down again into the bunker, a cellar several meters square giving onto a corridor closed by a grill.

The condemned men, who had had to undress in front of the barrack, entered their final resting place naked.

It was a place three meters square, empty except for a slop pail. At almost the height of the ceiling was a small barred window that diffused a vague light from the land of the living.

As the jailer closed the door, he jovially quoted them a line of a poem from his country: "You will dry out like tulips", he said.

Hunger is terrible; thirst is even worse. Dehydration attacks the brain cells first and unleashes silent storms of nightmares and hallucinations.

However, according to a former prisoner assigned to the bunker as an interpreter and undertaker who had, before dying in 1947, testified before a notary, Father Kolbe had no delirium and never complained as he grew weaker. He did his best to comfort his companions. When they went to take out the corpses, he was most often found standing or kneeling, praying or singing a canticle, repeated by the chorus around him. The witness, passing in the corridor, said that he thought he was in church. According to him, in the neighboring cells those dying from previous reprisals, who would soon reach the end of their agony, had the same impression, as did the prisoners in the courtyard of barrack 11 who sometimes saw the shaved heads in the moonlight and heard the singing.

The jailers themselves were astonished. "That is a man", they said.

Each morning they came to the bunker to empty out the slop and to take out the dead from the night before.

The oak door closed again on the pale beings already crossed off the register, who were no more than an ever more useless palpitation in their own tomb.

The fourteenth day, the vigil of the Assumption, the order was given to finish off the survivors.

A henchman of death armed with a syringe of phenic acid entered the half light of the cellar. He perceived three dying men stretched out on the cement and a dried-out figure folded against the wall. It was Kolbe, who had arrived at the end of his passion. The auxiliary approached him, and the syringe did its work.

"Then", says the Gospel, "the soldiers approached Jesus, and one of them pierced his side with a lance."

That is how Maximilian Kolbe died and with him the very pure child who had so loved the Virgin Mary. That is how the enthusiastic young priest who had written in his diary the resolution to give himself to others to the point of the supreme sacrifice died. That is how the prisoner who had once wished that his dust be dispersed by the wind died. By the eve of the Assumption he would be no more than ashes in the maw of the crematorium. Thus ended, in silence and abandonment, that life of which there remains nothing but love.